$10
c7961
CW01654438

aBsolutEly MaRdi gRaS

COSTUME AND DESIGN OF THE SYDNEY GAY & LESBIAN MARDI GRAS

DOUBLEDAY

POWERHOUSE PUBLISHING

First published 1997
A co-publication from Powerhouse Publishing and Doubleday

Powerhouse Publishing
part of the Museum of Applied Arts and Sciences.
PO Box K346 Haymarket 2000 Australia
The Museum of Applied Arts and Sciences incorporates the Powerhouse Museum, the Sydney Mint Museum and Sydney Observatory.

Doubleday books are published by
Transworld Publishers (Australia) Pty Limited
15-25 Helles Ave, Moorebank 2170

Transworld Publishers (NZ) Limited
3 William Pickering Drive, Albany, Auckland

Printed by Mandarin Offset in Hong Kong
Produced in Grotesque in Quark Xpress

Designer Colin Rowan, Powerhouse Museum
Editor Kirsten Tilgals, Powerhouse Museum
Photography Geoff Friend, Penelope Clay, Sue Stafford and Marinco Kojdanovski, Powerhouse Museum. Other photographers as specified.

National Library of Australia Catologuing-in-Publication data
Swieca, Robert
Absolutely Mardi Gras.

ISBN 086 824 682 4

1. Sydney Gay and Lesbian Mardi Gras. 2. Costume design - New South Wales - Sydney. I. O'Callaghan, Judith. II. Jones, Glynis. III. Title.
746.920994420

© 1996 Trustees of the Museum of Applied Arts and Sciences

This publication is copyright. Apart from fair dealing for the purposes of research, study, criticism or review, or as otherwise permitted under the Copyright Act, no part may be reproduced by any process without written permission. Inquiries should be made to Powerhouse Publishing.

Cover image: 'Pretty Pony' made by Michael Gates for Maude Boaté, 1995.
Pages 104-105: Remembrance Event, 1996. Photo by C Moore Hardy.

Acknowledgments

The generous assistance of the following individuals and organisations in producing this publication is very gratefully acknowledged:

ABC Television Documentaries and Features, David Abello, Danny Aboud, Australia Council, Terry Batterham, Rhys Butler, Martien Coucke, Fiona Cunningham, Noel Debien, Jamie Dunbar, Peter Elfes, Robert French, Larry Galbraith, Michael Gates, Lyndon Gaskin, C Moore Hardy, Gavin Harris, Brenton Heath-Kerr, Helen Johns, Vicki Jones, Craig Johnston, Bev Lange, Judy Martinez, Katrina Marton, Julie McCrossin, Ian McMillan, David McDiarmid, Gillian Minervini, Mother Abyss, Ron Muncaster, Dawn O'Donnell, Kimberly O'Sullivan, Cath Phillips, Philippa Playford, Githa Pilbrow, Leigh Raymond, John Robinson, Brian Ross, Mandy Smith, Ron Smith, the staff and board of Sydney Gay & Lesbian Mardi Gras, Jacques Straetmans, State Library of New South Wales, Sydney Star Observer, David Urquhart, John Webber, Bill Whittaker, Brendon Williamson, Garry Wotherspoon, William Yang.

Chapter 1

page one

Celebration!

by Robert Swieca

An overview of the polit

Robert Swieca works in education and visitor services at the Powerhouse Museum and was co-curator with Judith O'Callaghan of the exhibition *Absolutely Mardi Gras: costume and design of the Sydney Gay & Lesbian Mardi Gras* (6 February-21 April 1996). In addition to holding various positions within Museums Australia, he has been convenor of its policy committee on gay and lesbian culture in museum programs and practice.

Chapter 2

page thirtytwo

Outrageous! costumes & confections

by Glynis Jones

A look at what people wear in t

Glynis Jones is a curator of decorative arts and design at the Powerhouse Museum, specialising in contemporary Australian fashion. She has contributed to a variety of publications including *Decorative arts and design from the Powerhouse Museum, Australian fashion: the contemporary art, Christian Dior: the magic of fashion* and *Heritage: the national women's art book*.

d history of the parade

Chapter 3

page seventyfour

Glamour on a shoestring

by Judith O'Callaghan

A journey behind the scenes of the Mardi Gras Workshop

Judith O'Callaghan is senior curator of decorative arts and design at the Powerhouse Museum, specialising in contemporary Australian decorative arts and design. Her publications include *Treasures from Australian churches* **and** *Helge Larsen and Darani Lewers: a retrospective.* **She has also contributed to** *The dictionary of art, Decorative arts and design from the Powerhouse Museum* **and** *The Australian dream: design of the fifties*.

arade and why

Celebration!

by Robert Swieca

In the twilight of the first Saturday in March, gay men, lesbians and transgenders from across the city and across the globe assemble in Sydney. Organisations, groups and individuals come together on floats, in marching groups or as whimsical costumed entries. As the night progresses, the parade snakes its way between the crowds lining Oxford Street creating a colourful and joyous blend of music, movement and community pride.

The sense of fun and freedom brought by the night pervades the parade and its spectators. For one evening, the boundaries between revellers and onlookers, between queer and straight, are dismantled. In one sense, the community that celebrates Mardi Gras is Sydney itself...

Ooh, aah, it's Mardi Gras! The quintessential parade shot—lights, colour and movement. Fireworks explode over the Midnight Shift (a popular gay disco in Oxford Street) as the parade pulsates below.

Images of Mardi Gras parade through our memories. Who can forget the giant Imelda chasing her shoes down Oxford Street, the head of Reverend Fred Nile on a platter surrounded by the Sisters of Perpetual Indulgence, the advent of the all-girl and all-boy dancing troupes? Growing in size and diversity, the Sydney Gay & Lesbian Mardi Gras has transformed from march to spectacle; it has become a major cultural force. This month-long celebration is now the world's largest gay and lesbian arts festival. As a gay pride march, it is unique. Whereas other cities around the world hold marches during the daylight hours, in Sydney there is Mardi Gras—a night-time carnival, a wild celebration where serious issues are dealt with humorously.

The Mardi Gras festival is also one of Australia's most significant economic and tourist events, attracting thousands of people from interstate and overseas to Sydney and generating tens of millions of dollars. As attendance at the Sleaze Ball and Mardi Gras parties reach the 20 000 mark, and those for the parade zoom over 650 000, the question of these events mainstreaming also hangs from many lips. When ABC television first screened the parade in 1995, 40 per cent of the possible viewing audience tuned in. These national telecasts and the *Absolutely Mardi Gras* exhibition at Sydney's Powerhouse Museum indicate a climate of acceptance so different to Mardi Gras' radical beginnings.

What was punishable and reviled 20 years ago has now become acceptable and even fashionable! Why? How did Mardi Gras evolve? Well, in the beginning there was Stonewall.

Early on 28 June 1969, New York City police officers launched a 'routine' raid on the Stonewall Inn, a Greenwich Village gay bar. The police had little reason to expect trouble, since homosexuals rarely resisted them for fear of drawing further attention to themselves. But that night they began to protest loudly in the street, chanting GAY POWER! Several nights of confrontation sparked meetings and rallies and gave birth to a multitude of gay liberation groups. Stonewall came to be seen as the genesis of the modern gay rights movement with mythic significance.

The Sydney Gay & Lesbian Mardi Gras (SGLMG) had a no less tumultuous birth. The 1960s and 70s was a time of radical change in Australia: the war in Vietnam and the moratorium marches, Aboriginal civil rights, women's rights and the political upheavals of the Whitlam era meant that society's attitudes towards oppressed and alienated

Photo: Jamie Dunbar, 1993

'We play with the crowd and talk to the world through the parade.' David McDiarmid

Choreographed marching groups of boys, girls and drag queens have become an integral part of the parade in the 1990s. In the tradition of high camp, they have satirised traditional marching troupes, military salutes, Olympic athletes and even the idea of parading in costume itself. This group strutted their stuff to Kylie Minogue's Celebration— THE tune of 1993.

The first parade in 1978 was more like a protest march that turned into a near-riot as participants and police clashed. 'For gay men and lesbians to be doing it around a gay and lesbian issue—that is, our right to be on the street—was an exhilerating experience and very exciting.' Craig Johnston

Photo: Digby Duncan, 1978

groups were not what they were. For the gay and lesbian community, it was a decade of activism that was to culminate in the first Mardi Gras.

In March 1978, two Sydney gay activists received letters from the 'Gay Freedom Day Committee for Cultural Affairs' in San Francisco signed by Paula and Bud, a lesbian and a gay man ('Paula Bud' is not, as some thought, a full name). Was there any interest in celebrating an international day of gay solidarity to mark the tenth anniversary of Stonewall? The Sydney activists wrote to some 20 groups asking if they wished to take part. Out of this, the Gay Solidarity Group (GSG) was formed to organise a program of events and encourage interest in gay political activism. A street parade, complete with music, costumes and dancing, was one of the ideas put forward.

There are several interpretations as to why this form of activity was chosen. One of the organisers of the first parade later recalled that the GSG 'wanted a way to involve people in the streets that wasn't as confronting as a Saturday morning march where people's faces appeared on television. Something that would be a celebration of gay and lesbian freedom, a real celebration.'[1] Already some marches in the United States had a more festive atmosphere. Other people believed that the idea of masking one's identity in fancy dress was a good means of disguise (see Chapter 2). And there are those who saw it as a considered move to encourage political activism from a previously reluctant group.

'There was tension...between the bar scene—the gays and lesbians who went to bars—and the gay and lesbian political activists who were radicals. The Mardi Gras parade at night was a bridge, quite consciously, towards the scene.' Craig Johnston[2]

Whatever the reason, the celebrations were held on Saturday 24 June 1978. The first event, a morning march from Sydney Town Hall, was followed by a public meeting at Paddington Town Hall. Both events were well attended and when the evening parade and festival (as it was billed) began at 10.30 pm, between one and two thousand people took part.

The crowd chanted OUT OF THE BARS AND INTO THE STREETS! as it progressed down the 'gay-mile', the stretch of Oxford Street between Taylor Square and Whitlam Square where some of Sydney's gay night-spots were then located. However, it was at 11 pm, when the parade

'Mardi Gras these days is completely metamorphised. It's its own beast.' Brenton Heath-Kerr

reached the entrance to Hyde Park that trouble began. The police wanted the crowd to disperse but confiscated the lead truck and its public address system before an announcement to do so could be made. Chants of STOP POLICE ATTACKS/ON GAYS, WOMEN AND BLACKS! went up opposite police headquarters. Blocked from entering the park and still in a jubilant if somewhat confused mood, the crowd decided to continue 'and the only way was up'[3]—to Kings Cross, an alternative centre of gay life in Sydney. The atmosphere became more like a 1970s protest march. When the police wagons moved in and officers removed their identification badges, the crowd knew the confrontation was about to escalate. Fifty-three arrests were made.

> *'It was dykes who were at the forefront of the riot. They came from a strong tradition of feminism and street politics and street confrontations with cops, so they were the ones who took the risks initially. The queens in the initial riot were hiding under cars...throwing their hands up in the air, going "This is a nightmare"...The women had the strength.' David McDiarmid*[4]

> *'I'd gone along expecting a mardi gras and finished up in a humdinger of a riot in Kings Cross. Because of the police, it's grown to what it is today. Perhaps without that riot, we wouldn't have had Mardi Gras...It was terrifying. It was very violent.'* Peter Tully[5]

Reaction to this police action was both swift and long-lasting. Rallies, pickets and demonstrations took place all through that year and into the next, and over 100 other people were arrested. Eventually nearly all these charges were dismissed or dropped but not before a major Sydney newspaper had twice 'outed' those arrested, publishing their names, addresses and occupations.

> *'Sydney had its Stonewall moment, the necessary transforming moment, which galvanises and energises a people and a culture, and which makes great things possible.' Leigh Raymond*[6]

The legacy of that night was a bond between the gay and lesbian subculture and the political activists. Mardi Gras had become not only a political rally, it was equally suffused with the idea of 'community'.

The second parade would be a different affair with an even greater variety of events in the preceding week, including a film festival and a gay alternative fair in Hyde Park. The first 'dance party' was held as a fundraiser at the beginning of the week in Balmain Town Hall. Its style, with live music and a mobile disco, was that of the political left—more like a rather stagnant 21st birthday party than the hyper-staged ecstatic dance parties of the 1990s. Despite chilly relations with the authorities, people joined in and the atmosphere at the parade was

Designed by Chris Jones, 1978, collection of Mitchell Library, State Library of NSW.

The first Mardi Gras was organised as a gesture of international gay solidarity to mark the tenth anniversary of the Stonewall riots. The poster used 'butterfly' imagery, a popular symbol at the time to signify gay 'coming out'.

Designed by Sheona White, Lucifoil Poster Collective, Tin Sheds, 1981

Above: The first summer poster heralded the dawn of gays and lesbians stepping out to freedom and fun. It also advertised the availability of childcare—something that has not appeared at any Mardi Gras party since and a clear indication of how the night has changed in style and intent.

Photo: William Yang, 1981

Right: The first summer parade was about image rather than costume. It had enthusiasm and movement but not much colour. That was to come in 1983 with the influence of Peter Tully. In 1981, the moustached, T-shirted, macho men were more an assemblage of clones on the move than spectacle.

peaceful and fun. Some of the impact was lost, however, because of the lack of any organised activity at the end.

This would be remedied in 1980. The Gay Solidarity Group set up a separate task force with the purpose of organising events for Gay Solidarity Week, including the first post-parade party which was held at the Paddington Town Hall for 700 revellers. The idea of a post-parade party was also a merging of the two strands of community life that met in the parades. It was common in the 'gay movement' to hold some kind of dance or social function as part of a political event. In fact, gay and lesbian life in Sydney had a strong history of dances and balls such as the Drag and Drain parties of the thirties and forties and the Artists and Models Balls of the fifties and sixties. The seventies and eighties saw the Knights of the Chameleons and Family Balls while social groups such as the Boomerangs and the Pollys ran dances. It was not surprising that the idea of a Mardi Gras dance surfaced.

Despite the uneventful 1979 parade, the Task Group were still concerned that problems might arise and in 1980 they organised parade marshals and a bail fund in case of arrests. However, the only hint of violence occurred when a group of lesbian activists took exception to a perceived racist display on 'The Barrel Inn' float, surrounded it and attempted to board.

Although that year's Mardi Gras may have given the appearance of being fun—about one-quarter of the participants were in costume—there was friction. Some political activists saw the parade as purely a commemoration of Stonewall. Others, including those with commercial interests, saw it as a mass celebration of gay lifestyles. The former, marching in ordinary street clothes emblazoned with badges, dismissed costume and dressing up as a frivolous display which threatened to undermine and trivialise the message of gay solidarity.

These sentiments were in keeping with general attitudes towards fashion at the time. However, more recent interest in popular culture studies has seen the role of fashion re-evaluated. It is now recognised that the wearing of costume in Mardi Gras does not negate the political message of the event.

Of course, there have always been those who believed the parade could combine both fun and protest. In 1980, however, the differences in attitude found a specific focus. There was the suggestion that the parade be moved from winter to summer—an idea given impetus by the parade taking place on one of the coldest June nights on record. As Leigh Raymond quips, it had been 'decided perversely to hold a Mardi Gras, a parade held elsewhere to mark the end of summer, in the middle of winter'.

The Gay Mardi Gras Task Group began formal public debate on the issue.

'Those objecting mainly came from the political left, especially radical feminist lesbians whose argument centred on the fact that a winter parade would lend itself to a political gay rights demonstration which would not be diffused by popular or commercial interests. The strongest supporters for the change came from those who had been more involved in the camp subculture.' Craig Johnston

In the end, the summer option was accepted and with it the whole atmosphere of the event was transformed. The goals changed too, from 'overturning the patriarchal system' to law reform. As a result, lesbians, who were the core of the political movement, became far less involved and were marginalised within Mardi Gras. Many returned to the women's movement. It was a situation that was to last until 1988, one that impacted on the look of Mardi Gras by giving full reign to the male performance tradition of drag within the parade.

The Mardi Gras Task Group was reformed in 1980 as an elected and independent body. It had scant time to organise the next parade which was set for 21 February 1981. Then the party venue was mysteriously gutted by fire and it was only days before the parade that Hyde Park South, an outdoor venue, was locked in. When the appointed day arrived, the weather turned and the first washout occurred. The parade did take place one month later but the outdoor concert was not a success and re-inforced the need to secure an indoor dance venue. However, the increase in parade participants from under 2000 to 5000 provided tangible support for those who were trying to create an event with broader appeal. In the following year its scale grew further as organisers actively encouraged gay-owned businesses to become involved.

Ironically, politics emerged from the shadows for the 1982 parade. Mardi Gras was given a theme for the first time and the one selected for that year was 'On our way to freedom', a reference to the struggle for homosexual law reform.[7] It was a struggle bolstered by the growing attendances at the parade—over 10 000 lined the route—making it obvious that gay rights were not necessarily a fringe concern.

There were further innovations in 1983. A festival was re-established under the banner of 'Our lives/Our selves, a festival for lesbians and gay men'. And more significantly, the workshop was set up under the direction of Peter Tully (see Chapter 3). Tully was one of the few to have dressed for the first parade in 1978—he wore an American Indian outfit— and he was to have a major impact on the entire look and feel of future Mardi Gras.

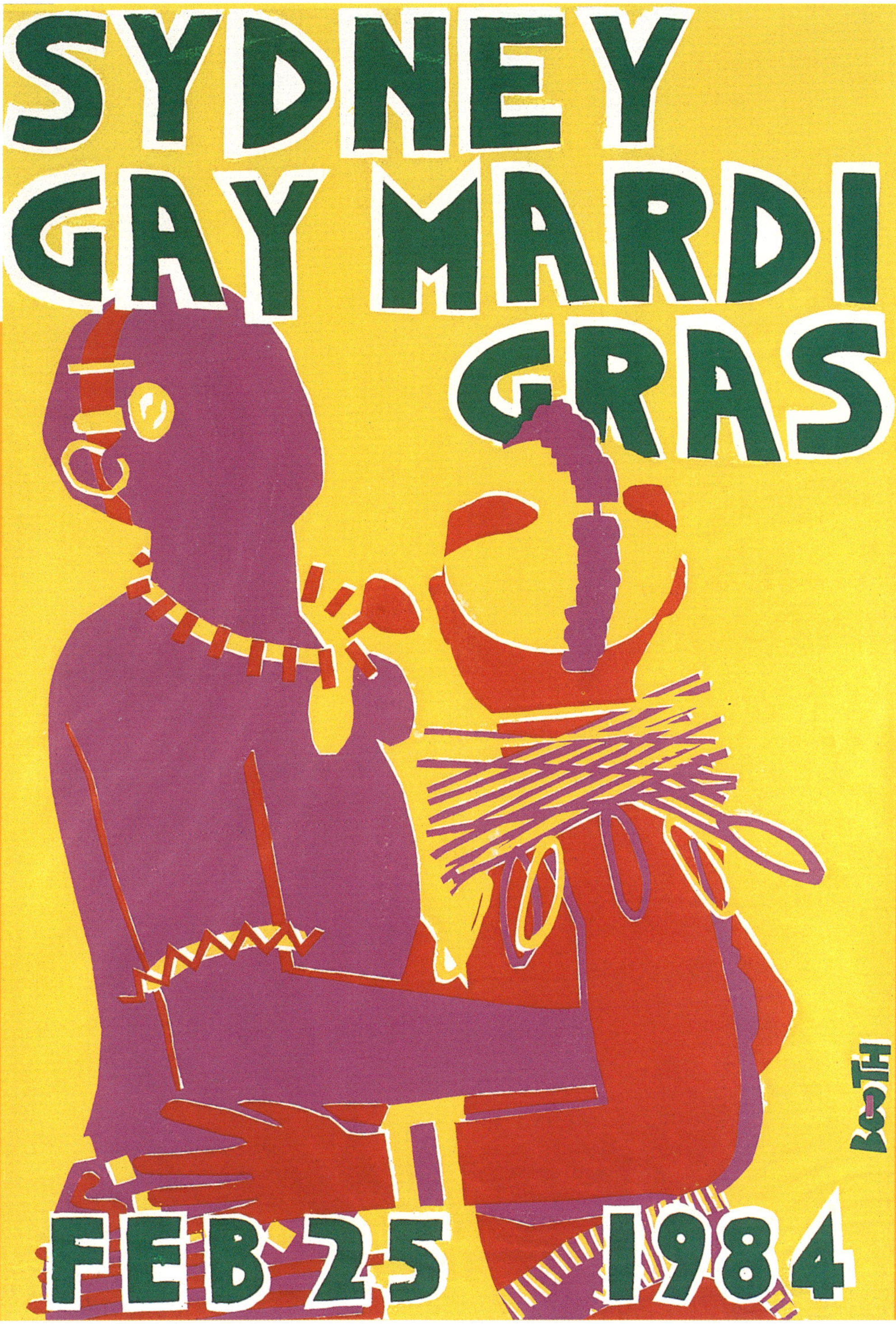

Designed by Allan Booth, 1984. Collection of Mitchell Library, State Library of NSW.

The 1984 poster captures not only the colours of summer—pink skin against the heat of the bright yellow sun—but also a tribal image, reflecting Peter Tully's idea that the gay 'tribe' was one of many that exist in Sydney.

The Mardi Gras parties are now phenomenal events. Amid music, floor shows, lighting effects and queues to the bathrooms, revellers dance on from parade-end until the stark light of morning. Those with energy to spare move on to recovery parties along Oxford Street.

'There is nothing else like it. There are other parades and things but they're a bit commercial, a bit safer, a bit more compromised, and a bit cliched.' Peter Tully

Photo: Jamie Dunbar, 1993

'Although I agreed with the issues, I didn't think it would last very long. Visually it had to be much more exciting and much more attractive for people to take to it in a big way. So we started working on the visual side of it to make it more exciting, a bit more interesting, dynamic.' Peter Tully[8]

Realising that they needed funds, the committee staged the first Sleaze Ball at Paddington Town Hall in September 1982 to raise money for the following year's Mardi Gras. The party theme, perhaps inspired by New York and Berlin parties of the 1970s and by a growing sense of sexual awareness, was a great success. However, it was clear that in future years a larger venue would be needed.

The Showgrounds had been booked for the party on Mardi Gras night in 1983; 6000 packed the AMP Pavilion. The gay press described the parade as an outstanding success but reported that the party (which was becoming as important to Mardi Gras as the parade itself) left much to be desired. To try to improve the situation, a more formal structure was adopted and the Sydney Gay Mardi Gras Association was formed.

The 1984 Sydney Gay Mardi Gras theme, 'We'll dance if we want to!', was chosen in response to police harassment of gay venues and their challenge to the 1983 Sleaze Ball's liquor licence application. In fact, applications for liquor licences were to cost considerable time, effort and money in the years up to 1994. This was a threat to the very existence of Mardi Gras which relied almost exclusively on the dance parties for funding.

The 1984 Mardi Gras party went on to be regarded by many as a watershed.

'It evokes the contemporary dance party formula—huge dance floor, music chosen for dance connoisseurs, drugs, sex and costume. It also suggests the male origins of Sleaze, and the meeting of...'clones'...and the 'style queens', who introduced to Mardi Gras the elements of dressing up.' Oxford Weekender, *16 September 1982*

Mardi Gras also relied on the new anti-discrimination amendments to get police and council cooperation for the parade. Crowd control was achieved by the use of marshals and, in later years, barricades. Considering the size of the crowd at 40 000, these measures were none too soon coming! They also had an impact on costumes, lifting previous restrictions on size and extravagance. The growing spectator numbers had made it hard for some of the participants to move up the street in large and lavish creations. They would arrive at the other end exhausted with their costumes in tatters. So, while the look of the parade benefited from these measures, the closeness and intimacy that hallmarked earlier parades suffered.

Although the parade audience had grown over the years to tens of thousands, the mainstream media still largely ignored the festival until 1984 when SBS television commissioned a half-hour documentary. Meanwhile, the Mardi Gras elections of that year returned no women to the board, reflecting an increasing gay male separatism in the growing crisis over HIV/AIDS.

As the community celebrated achieving homosexual law reform in NSW in 1984, the mainstream media began to cover the issue of HIV/AIDS in a sensational manner.[9] When Professor David Pennington, head of the AIDS Task Force, linked the post-parade party to 'a Bacchanalian orgy',[10] the Reverend Fred Nile of the Festival of Light (a fundamentalist Christian political group) took it as a call for the cancellation of Mardi Gras. There had even been discussion among the gay community as to the appropriateness of staging Mardi Gras itself, but these views were countered by parade coordinator Brian Hobday who described it as 'a much needed show of strength'.[11] The 1984 parade went ahead without problems, with an estimated 30 000 spectators and 8000 at the party.

This success along with the newly revived and expanded cultural festival made the 1985 Mardi Gras a ground-breaker. In the face of fierce opposition, it set the tone for years to come in terms of community cohesion and strength. A burst of activity became concentrated on Mardi Gras after the fight for law reform was won and this was reflected in the diversity of festival events including film, theatre, exhibitions, workshops and sport. The parade itself benefited as participants could feel liberated from the stigma of illegality while a new route made for a non-confrontational environment by avoiding the George Street cinemas, a likely Saturday night hangout for young homophobic men. In many ways, 1985 can be seen as the first of the contemporary-style Mardi Gras.

With a new management plan to improve efficiency, tighten financial control and reduce costs, the year would be labelled as the beginning of the 'professionalisation' of Mardi Gras. In subsequent years, the administrative reach of the organisation grew even greater, drawing criticism from those who saw the Mardi Gras moving away from its roots as a political event driven by volunteers and activists.

It was also the year of the first Showground 'concept party' for Sleaze—projects that would see the dance halls transformed into Mayan temples or littered junkyard landscapes. Dance attendees would dress to reflect the sleazy, sexually explicit nature of the ball. As a result,

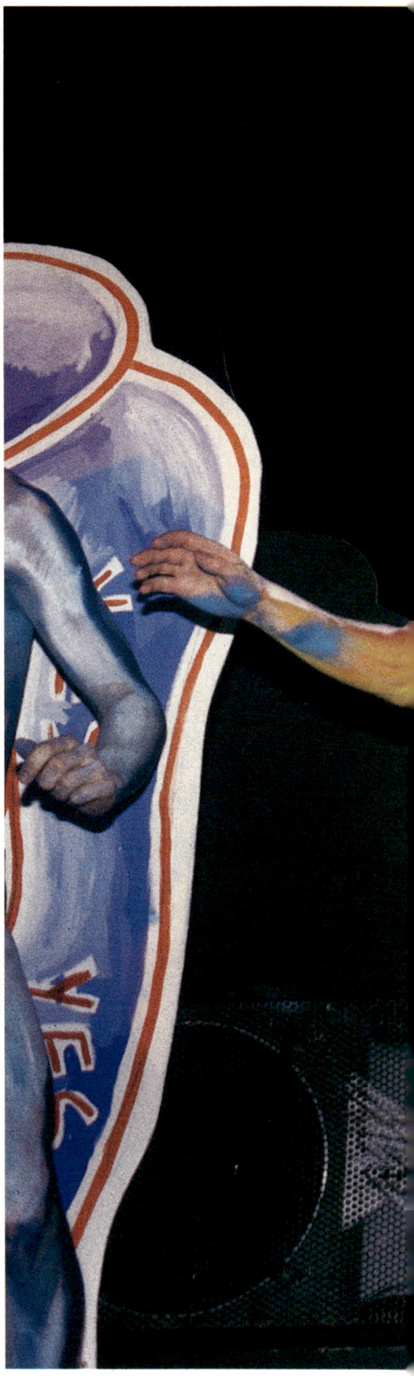

Photo: C. Moore Hardy, 1993

In 1992, the AIDS Council of NSW commissioned David McDiarmid to produce a set of safe sex posters. The following year these male positive/negative images were transformed into living three-dimensional figures for a parade float.

What was she thinking? (a) Was that a gun in his pants or was he just glad to see me? (b) If they're the Texas Rangers, I want to see the Mounties! (c) Bewitched, bothered and bewildered, am I. (d) Mmmmm, cream buns for tea!

Photo: Mervyn Fitzhenry

Photo: Jamie Dunbar, 1988

Aboriginal involvement in the parade was first seen in 1988 when dancer and activist Malcolm Cole lampooned the English 'discovery' of Australia by dressing as Captain Cook and standing in a longboat drawn along by white bearers.

the Sleaze Balls became giant extravaganzas, taking on an importance of their own.

The parade was also changing—the first Dykes on Bikes and Koori entrants participated in 1988 in front of 120 000 people. Lesbian involvement, although increasing, was still not as strong as it could be. With major gay groups 'going coalitionist', members of the Sydney Gay Mardi Gras Association voted to include the word 'lesbian' in the organisation's name. The change was too late to appear on the 1989 posters but the intention signified a wider degree of community involvement.

In the years since, the Sydney Gay & Lesbian Mardi Gras has had an extraordinary impact on the straight community as well. There has been a gradual (and sometimes grudging) acceptance of gay and lesbian lifestyles as valid parts of the city's cultural diversity. Gay men and lesbians, who for so many years were a subculture on the fringes of the

'Mardi gras is about something individual. It's about your own identity. It's about coming out. It's about who you are.' Philippa Playford

PRIDE (Sydney Gay and Lesbian Community Centre) is just one of many 'walking groups' that appear together in the parade out of a shared sense of purpose. This unity is reinforced visually through costume or by carrying flags, banners or props which may be used to communicate a specific message and to differentiate one group from another.

Photo: Peter Elfes, 1994

mainstream, are now often trendsetters for the rest of a youth-orientated society. As the differences between gay and straight in body image, dress, music, dance and other aspects of street and contemporary culture begin to blur, the issue of who you have sex with recedes in importance.

Gay men and lesbians have recognised the political and economic power in acting as a community, and have galvanised over the issue of HIV/AIDS. This has attracted an extra level of support from government, the police and the media throughout the year.

On another level, because it operates as a carnival or, as Umberto Eco writes, 'authorised transgression', Mardi Gras can only occur at a specific time and place. For one night, the queer community can suspend the control of the dominant culture, resulting in the dramatic expression of queer culture on the streets.

During the Mardi Gras festival, this is especially evident in the way Oxford Street is transformed from an urban thoroughfare to a processional way. Since 1990, flagpoles fly the Mardi Gras banners along the length of the route, while businesses decorate their windows and awnings with gay and lesbian imagery, utilising the rainbow colours of the gay and lesbian flag or creating variations of the Mardi Gras poster and theme for that year. In the week prior to the parade as the countdown begins, the excitement and energy along Oxford Street increases to a fevered pitch—ready for the explosion of sound, light, colour, glitz and glam that is Mardi Gras night.

The festival stakes its claims even further into spaces that were out of bounds in earlier times: Sydney Opera House, the Sydney Town Hall, the State Theatre, the Powerhouse Museum.

In doing this, Mardi Gras projects a minority image onto the mainstream by saying 'we have a right to be here'. Its very existence is a political statement of tolerance and acceptance, and it has played a major role in the definition of a gay and lesbian 'space' in Sydney by

Photo: C. Moore Hardy, 1996

These banners outside Sydney Town Hall symbolise the changing status of the Sydney Gay & Lesbian Mardi Gras. Once a pariah, it is now accepted by the general community as a valued part of the cultural life of the city.

The 1995 Sydney Gay & Lesbian Mardi Gras festival launch took place on the steps of the Museum of Contemporary Art near the spot where Captain Arthur Phillip proclaimed the settlement of Sydney in 1788. How would he have reacted over 200 years later to see Pierre et Gilles' poster boys and girls 'in the flesh', cavorting on a stage opposite the Sydney Opera House?

Photo: C. Moore Hardy

Fair Day has become a major community event in the festival. Community groups and businesses set up stalls and vie for attention from the throng of gay men, lesbians and transgenders, scantily clad in the humid heat of a February Sunday. The day's entertainment includes drag shows, sideshow rides and the ever-popular dog show for canine and owner.

Photo: C. Moore Hardy, 1993

'I think not everything is conservative, run-of-the-mill ...the world is full of fabulous, wonderful, crazy things. Life's too short to be really bland and boring, not open to differences.' Brenton Heath-Kerr

creating a territorial and symbolic centre for the community in the inner-city. In a way, it allows gay men and lesbians in Sydney to be visible throughout the year, rather than for just a period in March.

However, this acceptance of Mardi Gras has not been without its problems. With the increasing number of heterosexuals attending the parties, there was concern that the celebrations would be transformed into another avenue for popular—and thus straight, dominant—culture. In 1996 SGLMG members voted overwhelmingly to ask prospective new and renewing members to state their category of sexual preference. Applicants indicating that they are gay, lesbian, homosexual and transgender are admitted as a 'matter of right' while those in other categories must go before a membership committee.

The SGLMG has also developed its support role for gay and lesbian cultural expression. The re-invention is particularly evident in the posters for the parades. In the first three years, these were produced in the style of political handbills by collectives associated with the Tin Sheds at the University of Sydney. Early imagery of the 'coming out' butterfly dominated in the years of Stonewall commemoration. However, with the change to late summer, the posters evolved into more relaxed expressions of hedonistic enjoyment. Those of the early eighties flaunt and celebrate the parade, the party and sexuality while those in the later part of the decade reflect a movement towards inclusion and coalition. In the nineties, the posters and imagery have a more sophisticated, commercial graphic style, mirroring the change in production from a competition to a commission for gay and lesbian designers.

The board of the SGLMG now encourages the commercial potential of the event. Poster imagery has been adapted for the marketing of T-shirts, CDs, and coffee mugs, and the logo, title and the poster design are copyrighted by the organisation. SGLMG is now not only a political force but a corporate one too. Its operations include office and workshop space and a permanent, professional staff of more than 12. Statements of gay and lesbian identity writ large on the streets of Sydney do not come cheap and require planning, coordination and fiscal responsibility.

The Mardi Gras has fostered a competitive spirit of design and production and a display of creative endeavour that—although some may say tacky—is uniquely Sydney. These creations strut, whirl and line the streets of Sydney's gay space from Darlinghurst to Newtown and say with tongue firmly in cheek, 'We are what we are!' They have emerged from the Mardi Gras workshop and the spare rooms and garages of gay men and lesbians all over Sydney. There is also a Hall of Fame for significant contributions to Mardi Gras and an awards system which encompasses costume, floats, marching groups, walking groups and

Designed by Philippa Playford, 1992

Right: This was the first time the new title, the Sydney Gay & Lesbian Mardi Gras, appeared on a poster: it also marks the advent of a different style of poster design using computer graphics. The designer, David McDiarmid, had a close association with SGLMG, having been artistic director and a workshop artist for some years. He also designed the 1986 and 1988 posters.

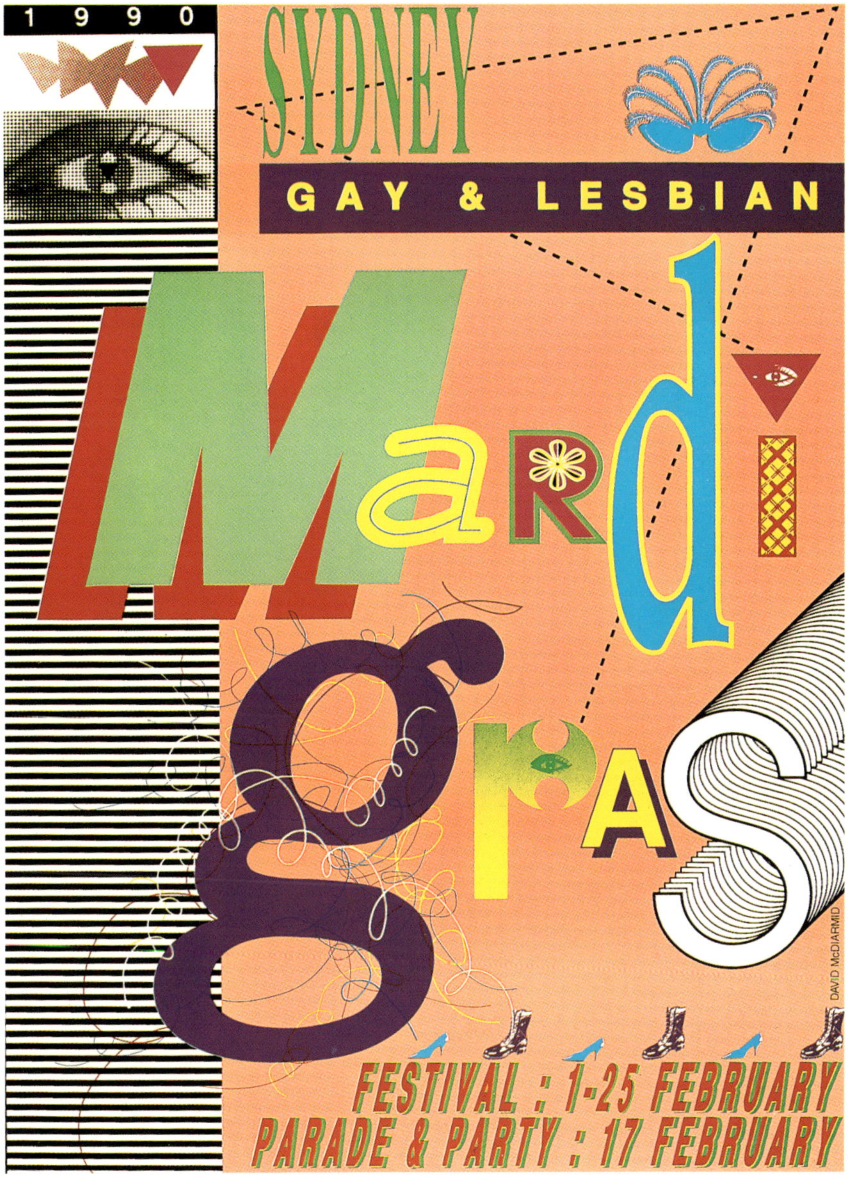

Designed by David McDiarmid, 1990. Reproduced with permission of the estate of the late David McDiarmid.

Left: The pink triangle, the rainbow colours of the gay and lesbian flag and a fulsome heart are ever-popular Mardi Gras images. They appear in 1992's playful poster and were reproduced in props and banners that year. The Sydney Gay & Lesbian Mardi Gras company logo appears on the poster; its inspiration—the Sydney Opera House sails and the pink triangle.

store-front and business decorations, and which also apply to other festival events.

Mardi Gras is many things to many people—parade, political statement, carnival, fiesta, a way to come out. For some gay men and lesbians, it's the equivalent of Christmas—a time for the community to come together and share. Whatever it is, it continually recreates itself, snubbing those who would wish to define its limits.

> *'I think of Mardi Gras as a month of celebration. We show our stuff to the world, gays and lesbians. Show how unique we are—and that's really special.' Philippa Playford*[12]

Designed by Pierre et Gilles, 1995. Posters on pages 26 and 27 reproduced courtesy of the Sydney Gay & Lesbian Mardi Gras.

In their customary style, Pierre et Gilles created beauteous air-brushed forms of gay and lesbian 'faeries' surrounded by flowers to reflect the elevation of Mardi Gras to almost 'divine' status as THE *international gay and lesbian event. At the same time, the waratahs—the state flower of NSW—claim the parade for Sydney. The flower motif made its way into the parade via the use of floral garlands that hung from the lead float.*

These stylised images of gay and lesbian identity were a success from the moment they were launched, appearing in store windows, on merchandise and as real figures within the parade. With them, 'unity within diversity' became the catch-cry of Mardi Gras.

Designed by Brendon Williamson and Darian Zam, 1996

Sydney Gay & Lesbian Mardi Gras timeline

1969

Stonewall riots, New York City.

Australia's first homosexual political organisation formed—ACT Homosexual Law Reform Society.

1975

South Australia becomes first Australian state to decriminalise homosexuality (in NSW, a 1976 bill is defeated).

1978

First government report on gay and lesbian lifestyles and problems published by the Royal Commission on Human Relationships.

A poll in *The Age* newspaper shows that 57% of Australians believe that criminal law should not treat homosexual and heterosexual law differently.

The Gay Solidarity Group (GSG) formed.

First parade with 1000-2000 participants, following a public meeting and march in the morning. There are 53 arrests.

1981

Outdoor venue selected for party. Rain causes first postponement.

Delayed parade with an attendance of 5000, starts in Flinders St, moves down Oxford and Liverpool Sts to George St and then up towards Hyde Park.

Private members bill proposing homosexual law reform in NSW is defeated.

1982

First theme for Mardi Gras: 'On our way to freedom'.

Anti-discrimination legislation passed in NSW.

First Sleaze Ball earmarked as a fundraising event for the following year's Mardi Gras. 700 attend.

Workshop established.

Over 10 000 spectators line the route from Sydney Town Hall to Showground for the 31-plus floats.

Over 4000 attend the party.

1970

hristabel Poll and John Ware found CAMP (Campaign Against Moral ersecution) and are the first gay activists to 'come out' in the mass media.

1971

First official public meeting of lesbians and gay men.

First gay and lesbian demonstration outside NSW Liberal Party headquarters.

1972

David Widdup becomes first openly gay political candidate, standing unsuccessfully for Federal parliament.

Sydney Gay Liberation Front formed. At its first demonstration, David McDiarmid becomes the first self-identified gay man or lesbian to be arrested.

1973

irst gay phone counselling service set up by CAMP (NSW).

emonstration against Dr Neil McConaghy, a leading aversion herapist.

ighteen gay men and lesbians arrested in Martin Place during he first nation-wide Gay Pride demonstrations. Australian and ew Zealand College of Psychiatrists declare homosexuality is ot an illness.

1979

New Public Assemblies Act makes march permits easier to obtain.

Parade becomes part of a Gay Solidarity Week. 1000-3000 participants parade from Taylor Square to George St and back.

The first dance party held as a fundraiser.

1980

GSG sets up separate task force to organise parade week.

Parade begins in Bathurst St with 3000 people moving along George St to Liverpool St, and then up Oxford St.

First post-parade party for 700 people.

Decision made to move parade to summer. Mardi Gras Task Group formed.

1983

Sleaze attracts 2500 party-goers.

Week-long festival resurrected for 83 Mardi Gras with the theme 'Our new gay dawning'.

Parade audience doubles to 20 000. There are over 40 floats and 6000 people at the party.

Sydney Gay Mardi Gras Association formed.

1984

'We'll dance if we want to!' Mardi Gras theme reflects the struggle over party licensing approvals. 8000 attend the party after a parade that featured 46 floats and a crowd of 50 000

Three openly gay men elected to Sydney City Council, ending previous council opposition to Mardi Gras.

First meeting of ARCONN (later ACON—The Aids Council of NSW).

Sleaze Ball held at Horden Pavilion for the first time, with 4000 people.

1985

First of the contemporary-style Mardi Gras with new parade route and wider festival events.

30 000 people watch and 8000 are at the party.

First Sleaze Ball "concept party" with 5000 in attendance.

Establishment of police/gay liaison group.

1986

Despite the rain, 60 000 watch the parade of more than 50 floats.

Sydney Gay Mardi Gras Association incorporated in NSW.

Committee decides to establish a more broadly representative Mardi Gras with the inclusion of more women, people of ethnic background and those from outside the 'gay ghetto'.

1992

Crowd jumps to 400 000 although party attendance steady at 15 500.

Seven members of NSW Parliament march in parade which halts for one minute's silence in rememberence of those who have died of HIV-related conditions.

1993

Half a million people watch the parade, then 18 000 attend the party.

Economic impact study released which shows that SGLMG festival and parade contribute $38 million to economy.

1994

A record crowd of 600 000 for the parade plus 19 000 at the party.

Over 16 000 at Sleaze.

1987

Mardi Gras becomes Australia's largest night-time event with a crowd of 100 000.

1988

60 floats including first Aboriginal float and first Dykes on Bikes in parade, watched by 120 000 people. There are 10 000 people at the party. Name changes to Sydney Gay & Lesbian Mardi Gras Association.

1989

Attendance at 200 000 with 15 000 at the party.

Fair Day begins.

Cath Phillips elected as first woman president of SGLMG.

1990

Even in the rain, 115 000 people attend the parade. There are 14 500 at the party.

Number of people at Sleaze now 12 000.

Board of management for SGLMG created to improve administrative and trading rights and to help in the enforcement of legal rights against copyright infringement.

1991

Crowd back up at 230 000 and 16 000 party-goers.

1995

ABC TV telecasts the parade while 150 000 line the route. The party keeps growing with 19 500 revellers.

NSW Labor Party endorses Susan Harben, an openly lesbian candidate and past president of SGLMG.

SGLMG begins to offer development grants to artists.

1996

Absolutely Mardi Gras exhibition at the Powerhouse Museum, Sydney.

SGLMG members vote to ask members to state sexual preference.

SGLMG launches Raw Nerve gallery.

Outrageous! costume & confections

by Glynis Jones

For the spectators, the most popular attraction of the Sydney Gay & Lesbian Mardi Gras is the costumes. While some may be simple, others dazzle with their extravagance or delight with their sharp wit and playful humour. More importantly, the costumes have become valuable tools for empowering gay men and lesbians, asserting difference from the straight community and at the same time, highlighting the diversity within that difference. They are also fabulous fun!

Brenton Heath-Kerr designed 'Gingham Woman' in 1991. 'It was for Sleaze Ball and I wanted to be visually unsleazy. I wanted to look like a sweet demure, fifties-come-forties, housewife. Then, by the nature of the character being so sweet, it was a really interesting juxtaposition—of having this fabulous-looking, sweet, innocent character in amongst this wild crazy sex party...Her influence has a lot to do with David Lynch, particularly Twin Peaks *and* Blue Velvet*—that combination of sweet and nasty.'*

Special
Kellogg's

Photo: Jamie Dunbar, 1990

'So I walked into the Mardi Gras workshop and spoke to David McDiarmid

When people think of the Sydney Gay & Lesbian Mardi Gras, they usually think of the costumes for these embody all the reasons for the parade itself: celebration, identity, community, creativity, fantasy, subversion and politics.

Among the colour and activity of Mardi Gras, the costumes must compete for the attention of the crowd and the cameras in the few moments that the parade passes by. As spectators, we are initially captivated by the glitz, glamour and humour but on reflection a more profound image reveals itself and we realise we have come away from the parade with more than just a visual high. Mardi Gras highlights the importance of clothing as a powerful and sophisticated communication system and what has been expressed here is a complex mix of personal, subcultural and community issues that ultimately affects our understanding of gay men, lesbians and transgenders.

We, at least initially, define each other by the image we present, and this image is one that we construct through clothing, makeup, hairstyles and body decoration. We even manipulate our physical form through muscle-building, diet and cosmetic surgery. So, while clothing expresses something of our individual personalities in an everyday situation, it is primarily an attempt—either consciously or on a more subtle level—to conform to some ideal, whether that be mainstream or subcultural.

Moreover, gay men and lesbians are very aware of, and often well practised in, constructing a mask of conformity. In the workplace, among biological families and on the street, identities have to be hidden behind a facade. This everyday 'disguise' can be a key to functioning in a society where discrimination is still a reality.

aid I wanted to make two lemons.' Philippa Playford

Philippa Playford and friend dressed as lemons for the 1990 parade, reclaiming a term that was schoolgirl slang for lesbians. 'My whole body was covered with the lemon, made out of papier mâché, with a chicken-wire frame. It was very cartoony—big cartoony eyes and puckering lips. We had little holes for us to see but the vision was pretty limited. We got knocked around a lot 'cause we couldn't see where we were going.'

In contrast, it is in the public yet safe space of the Mardi Gras parade where being queer (in all its permutations) is the norm. Here it is all right to display aspects of identity that may be considered 'unacceptable' in other public forums, to publicly express pride in being a gay man or lesbian. Here, costume becomes a liberating tool—both collectively and personally—where fantasies or hidden desires are revealed. The S&M, leather and bondage cultures can emerge from behind closed doors, and those who want to display their unclothed bodies can do so. This is particularly important for women who can express sexuality in the open without fear of verbal and physical attack.

Conversely, costume can also provide a way of hiding personal identity. This anonymity, particularly in the early days of the parade, allowed many to participate alongside other members of the gay and lesbian community without fear of recognition. For her first foray into the Mardi Gras parade, designer Philippa Playford constructed a costume in which she was completely encased.

> *'It allowed me to go into the parade and be a bit anonymous at first... I sort of dealt with my coming out through that experience.'*[1]

There is another kind of protection to be found in dressing up. Whether enclosing or notional, costume can liberate people from shyness and personal insecurity. Many participants in the parade speak of how the costume and the relaxed atmosphere of Mardi Gras provides a supportive environment for them to step out of the perceived limitations of their own personalities and bodies. By dressing up, they can adopt different masks that often say more about their true characters than does their day-to-day appearance. Like designer Ron Muncaster, many explore a bolder side of their nature:

> *'I suppose I'm bit of an exhibitionist and I like showing off, where usually I'm a fairly quiet person and I can't speak very well. This is one way of showing my personality—by dressing up.'*[2]

Dressing up also gives participants a chance to explore an alter ego. Designer and performance artist Brenton Heath-Kerr concealed himself within his costumes, literally from head to toe:

> *'Using mask and tribal costumes...was the perfect way to create a whole new character rather than expose yourself as an individual in a costume. I'd gotten to the point of actually creating a whole personality rather than being myself.'*[3]

With his new skin, his race, age and gender were no longer visible—the audience related only to the image of his adopted character. This gave Heath-Kerr a unique insight into how profoundly image, and gender in particular, affects our relationships with each other.

Parody is used to make political statements with humour. Increasingly these issues are not only of concern to the queer community but have broader public appeal. Local dissent was aired by the Faggots Against Runway Three (FART) protesting against the increased aircraft noise over Sydney's inner western suburbs where many gay men and lesbians now live. Likening it to the bombing of Hiroshima by the Enola Gay in World War Two, the costume portrays the 'battle zone' between government and citizens.

Drag queens come in all shapes, sizes and ages: some are old, some young, some gorgeous and flamboyant, some tacky and outrageous, some dowdy and demure. They have become an important part of the parade, adding glitz and quirky routines and engaging in witty repartee with the crowd.

'Spectacle is important—as are controversy, crossing boundaries of taste, loudness, irreverence, over-the-top behaviour, competitive attention-seeking, theatricality, glamour and glitz.' Ian McMillan

'The most interesting experience...is the way that other people react and treat you...I've had experiences being in a specific costume—the gold woman—where she was particularly glamorous and elegant, and people just treated me like I was some goddess. It was really different to, for instance, 'Tom of Finland', where here's this macho dude and everyone's sort of frightened of him.'

Photo: Jamie Dunbar, 1994

It is the camp sensibility with its meshing of humour and politics, its theatricality, and its subversion and inversion of the norm that has enabled costume to become such a potent force in Mardi Gras. In addition, objects and images from mainstream culture are twisted so that they take on new meanings for the queer community. In doing so, gay men, lesbians and transgenders can assert that social reality is constructed by the dominant culture and can be challenged and broken.

'That's the whole trick of costume, that's the whole aim of it: to confuse people.' Brenton Heath-Kerr

Philippa Playford's 'Cowdyke' costume is a clear example of how this process operates on a number of levels:

'It's very tomboyish drag. The hat's probably the most campy bit. I wanted to make a cowboy hat but have horns coming out of it so it's sort of like: is she a dyke, is she a boy, is she a cow?'

Playford, like many others, uses wit not only to upset expectations but to undermine the power of language. These days images and words that were once used to denigrate gay men and lesbians have been reclaimed by the queer community. By making them bold and larger than life and by using them over and over again, the original meanings have been invalidated and a new positive aspect has evolved. A group of men dressed as 'pansies' used humour to diffuse the derogatory connotations of this word as did the 'fairy' costumes of The Boomerang Social Club in the 1995 parade. Terms like poof, fag and lezzo are now proudly displayed on many costumes and floats.

Photo: C Moore Hardy, 1995

'The parade is an interface between the straight world and the gay and lesbian worlds where differences must be exaggerated for maximum effec

Above: The Lesbian Brides used their theme and dress to question the traditional concept of family. Appropriating items of clothing from both the bride and groom, they reassembled them into an outfit that reflected non-mainstream values.

Right: The once demure and self-sacrificing nature of the nun's wimple is exploded by Mother Helen Highwater of the Order of Perpetual Indulgence. Here, it is not only a glorious celebration of a church's soaring arches and crosses, but could also be a reference to a local centre for the worship of high culture, the Sydney Opera House.

The most visible example of this reclamation is the pink triangle symbol. Once used to mark homosexuals in Nazi Germany (as the Jews were marked by the Star of David), it is now used as a symbol of gay and lesbian pride. It provides a visual theme throughout the parade in a countless variety of forms, from the pink triangle loincloths of the Fag Flag wavers in the 1995 parade to an iconographic motif atop the headdress of one of Peter Tully's Mardi Gras costumes and the 'sacred pink pyramid' that was part of the 1994 lead entry.

But even within the community, the process of reclamation is not always well-defined. For example, three years after 'lesbian' was added to the title of the SGLMG, people were still very particular about labels. A group of women, including Philippa Playford, went dressed as cowgirls to the 1992 parade and found themselves very carefully described by the gay and lesbian media as 'lesbian cowpeople'. This issue was, in part, the inspiration for Playford when she created 'Cowdyke' and gave the old label of bulldyke a playful twist.

On another level, empowerment for lesbians and gay men is achieved by appropriating the ordinary or everyday from mainstream culture and subverting the original meaning—'a character in the wrong place in the wrong time' as Brenton Heath-Kerr puts it.

Within Mardi Gras the traditional concept of family is questioned through images such as lesbian brides in ultra-feminine tulle tu-tu's combined with gentlemen's top hats, and signs of power and authority are turned topsy-turvy when the business shirt and tie are transformed into skin-tight leather.

n McMillan

Photo: C Moore Hardy 1992

Similarly, some members of the Order of Perpetual Indulgence challenge conservative social forces through humour and parody rather than vitriol. They dress as nuns, making their own habits and adding quirky details such as the white potty seat Mother Abyss once wore as an elegant wimple. Favourites among both parade spectators and the queer community, the order actually began as a political group.

From within the Christian community itself, on the other hand, AngGays openly confronted the church about its bigotry while proclaiming their spiritual beliefs and sexual identity within Mardi Gras. This group of gay and lesbian Anglicans refused to be invisible and were not afraid to offend. Deliberately provocative, they mixed ecclesiastical robes with high heels to comment on the hidden sexual activity within church orders.

But it is not only the symbols of authority that can be manipulated with great effect. Even the most banal object or image can be used to reflect the tensions between the straight and the queer communities, between the dominant and the oppressed. A notable example is the whistle, traditionally part of the occupational garb of railway guards and the military and used to signal authority. By way of its association with anti-violence strategies it has come to signal 'blowing the whistle' on attacks against gays and lesbians. Now the whistle is a common 'accessory' among gay men and lesbians and is very much part of the sound of the parade.

Perhaps the most accomplished appropriator of the mundane was Peter Tully who took the ordinary and relocated it in his costumes and other artwork thus giving it new meanings and qualities. Frequently, he created the effect by massing objects—threading plastic forks into a wild fringe, for example, or stacking plastic kitchenware into a fabulous headdress. Sometimes the objects were chosen for their subcultural associations, such as 'amyl' bottles, keys, whistles and studs. In other instances, such as his leather-clad and studded 'shopping trolley' of 1990, he used embellishment to transform an object of domestic drudgery into an object of desire. His 1990 Mardi Gras costume incorporates all these approaches as well as a visual pun on the slang term for penis in the form of a large plastic bone hanging from an apron.

In Mardi Gras generally, not just objects but heroes are appropriated and can be given new connotations simply by being drawn into the queer community. Australians may hold the Aussie lifesaver as their ideal self-image—solid, dependable, decent, brave, independent, healthy—but he has also been absorbed into the gay iconography, the focus of an eroticised masculine ideal. He even forms part of gay greeting card series. Of course, given the fetishism of the muscle culture, it is hardly surprising that the lifesaver is a ubiquitous figure in the Mardi Gras parade.

One of the most enduring character costumes, however, among both gay men and lesbians is the cowboy/cowgirl. While the independence and resilience of the lonesome figure of the range may be the inspiration, it is more the urban cowboy that is the visual reference. The interpretation of this theme can vary widely, from the leather cowboys in chaps and g-strings to the marching cowboys and cowgirls in fringes, white satin and ten-gallon hats. Or then there is the parody of Philippa Playford's 'Cowdyke' costume with its cowskin-print shirt teamed with sparkling, hologram-trimmed chaps and fluffy, pink, hoof-shaped shoes.

Occupational dress provides an element of fantasy, possibilities for visual puns and the chance to get your gear off. Boys from the Bayswater Fitness Centre chose a stylish variation when they turned up in the 1995 parade dressed as lifesavers, marching along with their own 'waves'.

Photo: Peter Elfes, 1995

When the steroid-enhanced Chinese women's swimming team made news, a quirky variation of 'gender fuck' arrived at the 1995 Mardi Gras. Dressed in high-cut red swimsuits, these men with their hairy chests and moustaches not only looked incongruous but also showed up the artificiality of the team's 'masculinity'.

With her sensible shoes, handbag, gloves and floral frock, 'Miss New Zealand' epitomises one of the most popular and accessible faces of the parade—the character of the middle-aged aunt or 'old maid'. The presence of these icons of respectability within the parade delight with their familiarity and incongruity. They represent the 1950s world where 'all was as it should be'. In this instance, there is also another layer of parody—that of 'sophisticated' Australians mocking 'dowdy', 'behind-the-times' New Zealanders.

In fact, popular heroes of many kinds are parodied in Mardi Gras. This is often achieved through drag. However, at the same time drag can be used as a way of paying homage. One recent example is Clover Moore. Respect for this local politician who pushed through the anti-vilification bill in NSW was made visible in the group of neatly-suited and carefully-coiffured 'Clover Moore' clones who marched in the 1994 parade.

The Mardi Gras parade always features a plethora of characters drawn from history, literature, theatre, television and cinema. In part, co-opting these straight characters is a way of highlighting the invisibility of queer culture within mass culture. It also shows us that there are different ways of 'reading' these images other than that proposed by the dominant culture.

One of the most popular movie themes has been *The Wizard of Oz*, particularly as a play on the old euphemism for gay men, 'friends of Dorothy'. And there is a special appeal in characters that are already larger than life: the cocaine-snorting, Bolli-drinking, peroxide-haired good-time girl, Patsy, is the ultimate drag queen idol, and the babes of Melrose Place hold the same attraction—an exaggerated look and personality that translates well into street performance.

This gender transgression through cross dressing is one of the most common themes of the Sydney Gay & Lesbian Mardi Gras and also one of the most complex in its many manifestations. It is an integral part of many kinds of masquerade and carnival and has traditionally been an important element in gay and lesbian celebrations and parties.

> *'There's a long history of drag in Sydney. Maybe 'cause we're an ex-English colony'. 'And the vaudeville tradition was strong in Australia.'*
> *Peter Tully and David McDiarmid*[4]

For the glamorous drag queens and transvestites, drag can be a lifestyle or a matter of professional performance. In the early days of gay liberation, drag queens were seen as perpetuating the stereotyped image of effeminate men in frocks and thus politically incorrect. But then came 'gender fuck', when men wore frocks while very obviously retaining signs of their masculinity. Now the important place drag plays in the history and culture of the gay and lesbian community has been recognised. Rather than denigrating women, drag plays on the superficiality of sex role behaviour, revealing it to be an appearance that can be manipulated at will. Nor is the notion or popularity of drag confined to men. There is a female variation on gender fuck where women may don leather chaps, false moustaches and detachable penises, sometimes in a light-hearted parody of the clone phenomenon or sometimes as personal performance and role-playing.

'The lesbian community are the people who've really embraced all that gender fuck stuff...because I think that if gender has been used for oppression all your life, any destruction is going to be something that you're really going to embrace.' Kimberly O'Sullivan[5]

Again, Philippa Playford is one designer who has considered the implications of women and drag in relation to Mardi Gras.

'I think girl drag is different to boy drag...sometimes it's more fetish-bashed. Maybe it's not big and loud and fruity, it might be more of an internal fetish. We are still playing around with it. Not so much walking in a parade or miming to a song. We do it in a different way. I think through performance that girls are really starting to explore that drag side that they have inside them.'

At the other end of the scale, the over-the-top glamour and flamboyance of drag provide designer Ron Muncaster with a suitable medium for the creation of his large, elaborate confections. His 'Cotton Blossom' costume evokes the Hollywood glamour of actress Mae West but takes it to extremes with an enormous feather-trimmed hat and masses of tulle and sequins.

While Muncaster would not consider his costumes political, his designs are aimed at a straight audience with the purpose of building acceptance by lifting the awareness of the queer community's creativity:

'We get smiles from the crowd. They mostly clap when they see us, and it really gives me a buzz to see it because they seem to like it. I like that contact with the straight crowd. If I am not being too outrageous, if I can be something they admire, then it helps the relationship.'

'I've been in absolute agony walking in that parade.' Ron Muncaster

'I thought my costume looked sort of southern so I'll call my costume "Cotton Blossom", because it was all white and frothy.' It won Ron Muncaster the judges' prize for excellence at the 1994 Mardi Gras. The effort he puts into costumes like this is incredible. 'I spent about three months on the sewing machine sewing all these frills and making all these roses and my wrists got so sore I couldn't sew any more...I mean there was seven metres of tulle in one small flower which had to be trimmed with sequins and then gathered on a machine and then sequins sewn in the middle.'

BE

Photo: Peter Elfes 1995

Above: The smell, the feel, the look of leather and rubber yield a variety of erotic experiences. For the onlooker, the appearance of the Leather Pride group in Mardi Gras hints at hidden rituals and pleasures.

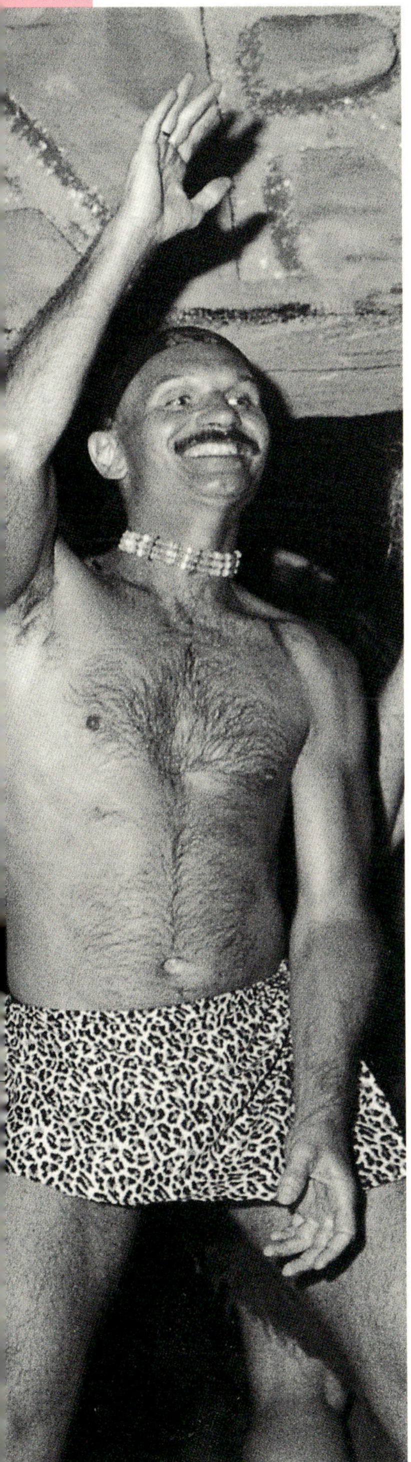

Photo: Chris Pavlich, 1994

Left: Hairy and proud of it! The Bears are a group who refuse to be forced into the popular mould of the gym-pumped body. Associating themselves with the Stone Age they go back to the roots of masculinity before hair was simply something to be quickly waxed away.

In addition to using costume to subvert the norms of the wider community, it is also used by subcultures as a way of actively claiming their identity within their own community. The clothing worn by many participants in the Mardi Gras parade is their *sub*cultural dress. While they may or may not wear it in public, it is still a part of their everyday lives. The club scene, for example, has generated a look based around figure-hugging, Lycra clothing. This look is peppered through the parade but has its greatest impact when seen on mass. Other groups such as Leather Pride promote the leather lifestyle in costumes that are part Marlon Brando and part urban cowboy mixed with the accoutrements of S & M. This raw hyper-masculine look, while defying the straight stereotype of the effeminate gay, has more recently been subverted from within. In the 1995 parade, for example, a man led the Leather Pride group wearing a delicate lacy coat over his leather.

Dykes on Bikes also have a complex iconography of dress. They take some of the traditional emblems of masculinity—hard black leather and the motor bike—and mix them with lingerie, fetish pieces and bondage items to celebrate the hidden areas of their sexual experience and the ambiguity of feminine/masculine roles. Lesbian stereotypes are challenged as women with shaved heads and tattoos appear wearing frilly party dresses.

Such layering of signals is common and not always meant to be decipherable outside a particular group. While, for example, tattooing, piercing and bondage can be read on the surface as erotic in intent, to those in the know the images communicate more specific sexual preferences.

Another way of actively claiming identity is through the use of 'national' costume. For a number of years Aboriginal gay men and lesbians have sought to make an identifiably Koori statement in the parade through costumes and floats that use a mix of contemporary and traditional imagery.

> *'Expressing our sexuality is as important to us as expressing our culture. We are part of the gay and lesbian community as well. We want to be visible. We want to be accepted as well.' Vicki Jones, from the 1995 'Everybody's Business' float*[6]

Gay men and lesbians of Asian heritage may have a complicated relationship to their cultural background, with many estranged from their own ethnic communities. As these communities are often extremely conservative, the individual's experience of being out about their sexuality can be very liberating. They are able to use costume from their ethnic background to assert their identity and make a space for themselves within the predominantly Occidental gay and lesbian environment. In fact, often these costumes are among the most spectacular in the parade. Some draw on the long history of female impersonation within traditional forms of performance.

Dykes on Bikes appear at the head of the parade in a variety of looks that challenge preconceptions about gender, lesbians, femininity and sex. Body decoration in the form of tattooing and piercing is often an important and permanent part.

Photo: C Moore Hardy, 1995

Right: The participants on the Aboriginal float wore a complex mix of costumes and body decoration inspired by the history of their indigenous communities. In particular, the translation of rock art into a kind of second skin is a very effective and potent symbol of community pride.

Below: Ethnic traditions are a rich source of inspiration for Mardi Gras, particularly among participants of Asian heritage. The flower image used in this costume is full of meaning: the hibiscus is a Chinese symbol of fame and riches and also refers to a young woman's powers of attraction.

Photo: C Moore Hardy, 1994

For the women who took part in the 1995 Asian Lesbian Wedding float, dressing in traditional Chinese robes represented a re-interpretation of an archetypal Chinese wedding. Two families were represented as being joined together, rather than one family giving away and the other receiving. As one of the women involved with the float explains:

> *'Basically in Asian society, women either get sold into marriage or slavery. We had the idea of breaking all those stereotypes... We used all the traditional symbols: dragons representing [male] strength, the phoenix representing new birth.' Happy Ho*[7]

On another level, national costume as fancy dress has been popular since the masquerades and balls of the 18th and 19th century. Although the outfits of these times may have been inspired by colonial attitudes, there were also the romantic associations of picturesque locations and exotic peoples. Such flights of fantasy are still found in Mardi Gras. Ron Muncaster's 'Arabesque' costume, for example, is a highly fanciful adaptation of Arab dress in the Hollywood tradition. Egypt has also provided a rich source of inspiration for many participants; the loin cloth is one of the most popular forms of dress in the Mardi Gras, providing an easy visual reference and enabling the baring of much flesh.

Right: Some Mardi Gras ensembles are elaborately planned and conceived. The gorgeous 'Orlando' float in the 1995 parade was one of these. It was based on the Sally Potter film of Virginia Woolfe's book which depicted a character who transforms from man to woman.

Below: Historical dress from the 18th century is one of the favourite themes of Mardi Gras, the elaborate skirts and hairstyles providing ample opportunity for exaggeration. This group in the 1995 parade took the pannier skirt and reduced it to its simplest form, divesting themselves of the bodice to reveal well-toned chests, adding hats that resemble baby bonnets and stretching the skirts to their widest proportions.

'You are creati

Photo: William Yang, 1995

mething that represents YOU: your gorgeous ideals, your bitchiest humour, or your most powerful politicalstatement.' Guidelines for floatmakers

Photo: William Yang, 1995

The tradition of fantasy was taken up in another way in Mardi Gras by designer Brian Ross. In Ross's work, a different carnival theme is evident. He created animal costumes that are large yet live—lobsters, birds and fish—and that work as street theatre rather than party outfit.

In fact, the choice of costume for the Sydney Gay & Lesbian Mardi Gras parade provides a tangible link to the many other forms of masquerade and carnival that have gone before. There are many themes that remain perennially popular, whether drawn from the Venice Carnivale or the more recent American street parades such as the New Orleans Mardi Gras and the Greenwich Village Halloween parade. In Sydney, however, they have taken on their own flavour.

> *'Trinidad, Rio, South Pacific festivals. We've always been strongly influenced by Third World sort of festivals. And Bali—they are big on ceremony. So [we had] the opportunity to use that, with the history of drag shows and that sort of gay aesthetic.' David McDiarmid*

The connections can be drawn even to 17th century masquerade in Europe. There, reversals of gender and social roles were also common themes—men dressed as old women, duchesses as milkmaids and gentlemen farmers as sailors. Or they wore the all-enveloping cloak and mask known as the domino. Like today, parodying political figures and social events was part of the fabric of the occasion.

The anonymity that costume provided broke down the normal social divisions between rank and class, occupation and race which led to a mood of social and moral freedom and a liberating and sexually-charged atmosphere. It is this spirit that still resounds in the Sydney Gay & Lesbian Mardi Gras.

Over the years dressing-up for the Sydney parade has actually meant less dress as more body is exposed. The marching and dancing groups, in particular, use choreographed routines to proudly show off their physiques. Often representing gym clubs, they display bodies that reflect an ideal of physical beauty, both straight and queer. The firmly-toned, pumped-up and hair-free bodies can be seen as a 'costume' in themselves; they are not the 'natural' body form but are part of an image carefully constructed in the gym and the beauty salon. It is an image that has taken more time to create than any sewn and glued costume, involving hours of working out, waxing and tanning.

Some participants in the parade flaunt their bodies in an even more blatant manner, more interested in provocative sexual display than narcissistic pleasure. Almost every Mardi Gras outfit can provide a chance for disclosure—by misplacing part of the clothing or replacing it with a new suggestive part. Historical, particularly 18th century, costume

'In the early days it was very risque to go out on the street dressed up in outrageous costumes, and Mardi Gras gave us the opportunity to do that... Having a crowd of people all dressed up gave us the courage, whereas we wouldn't have done it on our own.' Ron Muncaster

'Lucille Balls' won first prize in the 1994 Mardi Gras awards. Designed by Ron Muncaster and worn by his partner Jacques Straetmans, it highlights the often obscure sources of Muncaster's inspiration. 'People wonder where I get my ideas from and I get them from strange places like walking through BBC Hardware...This year I was walking through a haberdashery and I saw all these polystyrene balls in different sizes so I thought that's an idea, I'll make a costume made out of balls...I used over 200 balls. It took weeks and weeks to stick all the sequins on.'

Next page: The pumped-up muscles of these men and slim sensuality of the women explicitly counters 'straight' stereotypes of effeminate men and butch dykes. The body-painted group formed part of the lead entry for the 1995 parade.

is a popular theme: breasts are pushed up or uncovered, and panniered skirts lose their petticoats, exposing legs. Worn without trousers, cowboy's chaps reveal naked buttocks.

With such an emphasis on the body beautiful, there are those who want to counteract what they perceive as a stereotyped and discriminatory image. Groups such as the Vintage Males and The Bears offset the emphasis on youth and beauty by baring bodies that are far from these standards. Brenton Heath-Kerr's work developed from this starting point and his 'Tom' costume with its hyper-masculine physique was a comment on the superficiality of this constructed image.

> *'I was actually shy of my body and I didn't really fit in with that whole dance party scene, a la taking off clothes or shirts and being sweaty or particularly basely sexual. So I started out of a sense of insecurity more than anything and then, as it developed, obviously this insecurity turned into a security...' Brenton Heath-Kerr*

No matter what the specific issue that an individual may explore, an important facet of the parade for all the participants is the relationship with the crowd, for whom they are performing afterall. To feed off the adulation, becoming for an instant the centre of attention, loved and cheered, that for many is the moment worth waiting all year for.

'Over the years the whole principle of masks has been used for streng and for fear and for power—all sorts of conjuring.' Brenton Heath-Ke

Brenton Heath-Kerr translated the illustrated cult-character 'Kake' by Tom of Finland into a life-size animated being. Rather than celebrating the myth, the flat quality of the costume and its stilted movements parody the body culture associated with the gay club scene. 'I wanted to make him a two-dimensional figure to emphasise the fact that he's all surface, there's no substance in the image'. The costume comes with interchangeable faces and a detachable penis. 'Tom' was awarded second prize at the 1992 Mardi Gras costume awards.

Philippa Playford

'I happen to be a lesbian but the style of what I do has a campy quality.'

Glass and mixed media artist and designer Philippa Playford joined the Mardi Gras workshop as a volunteer in 1989 and worked from 1990-1992 as a workshop artist. 'I watched the '88 parade and it really inspired me. I thought, "I want to be in the parade. I want to work with other artists and make things".'

Her experience of the workshop affected her personally and professionally, freeing up the camper, more humorous side of her personality, enabling her to express her sexual identity through her artwork and opening her to the possibilities of a wide range of non-traditional materials. She no longer feels bound by traditonal concepts of art. 'I really enjoy making props and sets and working in lots of different materials. I certainly don't feel bound by any one. I am not a purist by any means, so I find the material that will relate to what I'm doing.'

While at art school Playford developed the bright colours and cartoon imagery that have become hallmarks of her style. The humour, exaggeration and larger-than-life characters that are such a familiar part of children's iconography in Playford's hands become an almost endearing way to communicate serious issues in an accessible and non-confronting manner. She also acknowledges a religious edge to her work. 'Being brought up Catholic has had an influence on my work, the detail within some of the artwork, the gilt frames and chintziness, I really like that.'

Quite a lot of time is spent just thinking about what to wear at Mardi Gras. It is very important to her that the costume has a political idea behind it. 'I am really interested in using labels which empower me and also other gays and lesbians'. By maintaining a sense of fun, she ensures the audience can relate to it as well. Playford understands the momentary nature of the parade where there is a lot of competition for audience attention so she prefers to make a bold statement rather than concentrating on fine detail, recognising the crowd won't notice a few sequins out of place. Once the idea is clear in her mind she works quite quickly to make the costume: 'Cowdyke' was made in a week to a strict timetable for the completion of each piece.

The Mardi Gras parade is very important to Playford: it allows her to assert her identity and explore her creativity. When she gets into her costume, she can play around with the ideas of girl-drag and the exhibitionist within her is let loose.

Opposite: Philippa Playford re-interprets the traditional lesbian drag image of the tomboy cowgirl in her costume, 'Cowdyke' which won the inaugural award for best costume worn by a woman in the 1995 Mardi Gras. It mixes and subverts popular symbols of masculinity and femininity. The power of the horns is undermined by fake fur and tassels similar to those worn by showgirls on their nipples. The innocence of the kewpie doll is questioned by the provocative draping of pearls.

Peter Tully

'Art should be for everyone....people get intimidated by art. It should be part of our daily lives instead of something we go and see once a week'

Peter Tully melded art, life and politics. He would garnish his poached eggs with nipples, encrust a domestic iron with jewels and celebrate gay sex through his creations, subverting notions of good taste, morality and art.

Tully was undoubtedly the most influential designer involved with the Sydney Gay & Lesbian Mardi Gras. Through his role as artistic director from 1982-1986, he played a major part in the parade's transformation from political march to cultural event. The Mardi Gras workshop was founded under his direction in 1982-1983 (see Chapter 3).

During the seventies and eighties Tully worked with designers Linda Jackson and Jenny Kee, producing jewellery that drew on Australia's natural and cultural environment. His experience of traditional tribal cultures through many years of travel in New Guinea, Africa and India—along with the vibrant and creative urban sub-cultural 'tribes' he saw New York—stimulated the development of his 'urban tribalwear'.

He once said of the legendary Paradise Disco hotel in New York City: 'It was about 85% black and very exciting. They played the best music I'd ever heard and the people dressed. Even though they didn't dress expensively, they had lots of style. They could wear a paper bag and look like a million dollars. And they really impressed me. So that was the impetus to get into costume.'

Inspired by the way tribes created an identity through their ceremonial or party costumes, Tully was determined to create a cultural identity for his own gay tribe on his return to Australia.

Distaining the elitism of the art world, its precious attitudes and materials he became a master of transformation, using the most mundane and kitsch of modern materials and found objects: dayglo plastics, fake fur, trinkets and cheap toys. By combining them in unexpected ways, and drawing directly on the imagery of popular and gay culture, Tully could transform the ordinary into spectacle.

Best known for his extraordinary jewellery and costume designs, his range of production extended from small and intimate works to major public events such as World Expo 88.

Peter Tully died in Paris in August 1992 from an AIDS-related illness. He was 45.

Opposite: Peter Tully transformed everyday objects into a costume of ceremonial proportions for the 1990 Mardi Gras, where it won second prize. A strong example of his 'urban tribalwear', its apron is made up of the detritus of the industrial world: broken watches and audio headsets, machine-made lace, a biscuit cutter and toy iron, leopard-print shoulder pads and plastic cutlery. These discards appear 'precious' when part of this spectacular costume.

Brian Ross

'I can do as I want, make what I want. It's very challenging; it's something I build up to each year. I put a lot of effort into it and I see if I can do better than last year.'

Brian Ross began making himself costumes for Mardi Gras in 1982 and, with his complex and unconventional designs, became one of its major prize-winners. He furthered his involvement in 1988 by joining the Mardi Gras workshop as an artist, designing and making floats and props for the parade and dance parties. His primary motivation was a desire to explore his creativity, although there was also the buzz he felt from an enthusiastic audience reaction. The combination of his disciplined and finely-tuned skills with the freedom and energy of Mardi Gras was a liberating experience for Ross, both personally and professionally.

Reflecting his background in graphic design and architectural model-making, Ross's costumes were more constructed than made and he always worked from a strict set of drawings. He preferred not to draw on traditional Mardi Gras themes or drag for his designs but to create something individual. 'What I like to do is something completely different to Rio. There is a lot of representation of feathers and sequins, and I believe we can use other things that are just as entertaining.'

His costumes were always bold and unconventional. Animal themes with a twist were a favourite as were futuristic creations such as his galactic headpiece with flickering brain.

Ross was particularly interested in finding and experimenting with new materials, including 'all sorts of toxic plastics'. The parade milieu influenced his choice. He painted 'Lobster Mornay' in fluorescent colours to catch the night lights. Similarly, the reflective surfaces of 'Man-Crab' were covered with holigraphic paper.

Brian Ross died of an AIDS-related illness in 1994. He was 46.

Opposite: The idea for this 1994 Mardi Gras costume came from an image on a restaurant menu which Brian Ross translated into three-dimensional form. To ensure the shape would fit, he drew a silhouette of himself on a wall over which he superimposed an acetate outline of the lobster. 'I think the stiffness of it gives it that toy effect I wanted to achieve. It's almost like a piece of meccano.'

Ron Muncaster

'I've been an antique dealer for 30 years and this little costume thing is just a little hobby of mine'

A major obsession would be a more appropriate description of Ron Muncaster's 'little hobby', designing and making costumes for himself and partner Jacques Straetmans (who died 29 January 1996) to wear in the Mardi Gras parade. They are the culmination of almost a year's thought, four to five months' work and hundreds of dollars in materials. Muncaster is one the most prolific and memorable of the costume competition entrants, receiving more awards than any other contestant—eleven prizes, including six firsts, in eleven years.

The adulation of the crowd and the opportunity to be creative are the source of both his motivation and his continuted enthusiasm. Although now 60, his passion has not diminished: 'Retire! I'll never retire, I said, even if they have to wheel me up on a float, I'll still be there in the parade because it's the highlight of my year.'

His home is his workshop, an Aladdin's cave with entire rooms taken over by costumes, past, present and in progress. The labyrinth of small spaces and staircases has forced him to design the huge costumes so they fold or dismantle.

Muncaster has no training in the design and construction of costumes. 'I first started by buying a paper pattern but I didn't know how to read the pattern because it looked so complicated. I just ended up cutting the shape out myself. It's all trial and error...This is where I sometimes get into trouble. I have these ideas but I don't know how to construct them...When I come to get it all together, it doesn't turn out and it ends up something else.'

Nevertheless, his creations are finely detailed and finished. They are always elaborate, fanciful pieces very much in the tradition of the Carnival in Rio and New Orleans Mardi Gras. The sheer magnitude of each costume is startling, especially in relation to Muncaster's almost fragile physique. However, he has refined his techniques and materials to produce large but lightweight sculptural forms. In fact, the materials are often the starting point for a design. Hardware, haberdashery and sports stores have all provided a disparate mix of objects that have sparked his imagination.

'It is the artistic side of Mardi Gras that I like.'

Opposite: Mardi Gras costume is all about illusion—the audience can rarely recognise materials due to the lighting and movement of the parade. In 'Arabesque' Ron Muncaster has made extravagant arm decorations from placemats and ping-pong balls, and the curly-toed boots are actually rubber galoshes customised with sequins. Muncaster designed it for Jacques Straetmans for the 1992 Mardi Gras where it was awarded best costume.

Michael Gates

'I was introduced to my first pair of heels and I never looked back'

Michael Gates, like many other gays, spent his younger days enduring the taunts of his school peers. His current success as a drag performer compensates for the years spent trying to deny his desire to dress from his mother's wardrobe.

As Maude Boaté he has wowed Sydney audiences with exuberant shows which he also directs and produces. His character draws partly on the dry wit of his idol, the actress Bea Arthur, and Auntie Mame with her cry of 'live, live, live'. It was being diagnosed as HIV positive that led him to 'get the finger out' and start doing what he wanted.

He describes himself as the 'mother' of a new generation of drag performers. Unlike the 'hormones and tits', grace and glamour of the old queens, he sees the new generation as 'just guys dressing up to have fun and a job'. The presentation, while still glamorous, has more in common with the makeup and humour of traditional clowning. The characters depicted by Gates are drawn from Hollywood movies both old and new, so leading ladies from the 1950s sometimes find themselves with a sci-fi twist.

Gates is also known for the 'big wigs' he creates for his shows and to wear at parties and Mardi Gras. He sat atop the 1994 ACON float, a commanding figure in a 'helmet' headdress he titled 'St George'. His 'Hare Hare' headdress was worn by Boy George when he was the surprise guest at Mardi Gras in 1995, although Gates didn't know this when he made it.

The wigs originally evolved out of necessity because commercial wigs were very expensive and budgets for the shows tight. Gates started out with a block of polystyrene and a bread knife and progressed to working with moulded latex and plastics. Their sculptural forms and zany colours gives the wigs a cartoon quality

In recognition of his outstanding contribution to the art of drag, Gates won five prizes at the 1996 DIVA (Drag Industry Variety Awards), including best costume design and best show.

Opposite: 'Tomato Head' was made for Maude Boaté for a drag show in 1994. It was constructed with spray paint, hot glue, papier-mâché, sponge foam and latex.

Photo: John Webber

Opposite: *Brenton Heath-Kerr extended the life of his characters through photographic postcards, enjoying the unpredictability of where the images might eventually be found. 'I've done a series of postcards. The really bizarre principle is that you don't know where they've been sent to. I could*

Brenton Heath-Kerr

'The nature of the disease means your life is shortened and this concentrates your creativity and passion and the urge to express yourself honestly...I've realised I wouldn't have created any of my work if my path had been different.í

It was Heath-Kerr's HIV positive status that led him to re-evaluate his life, stop working in 'straight' jobs and explore his creativity. He began by making 'little, fun, sort-of-light-up things—spinning gadgets' to accessorise outfits but it was his insecurity with his physique that initially led him into making entire costumes, ones that enclosed the body completely. He began to explore how people are 'read' through image, commenting on how much importance society places on this reading yet how superficial and unreliable it can be.

'My reason for covering the whole body, face, hands and usually I only leave the eyes...is that I want to express the human being as actually any image. It's just a shell and principally we're all the same underneath ...Differences are surface. They are what we do, not who we are.'

Heath-Kerr's costumes involve complete characters although the actual personalities are developed only with the wearing of the piece, a strange experience in itself. 'I make everything pretty fitting and, with the nature of mask, you experience a whole sense of suffocation but then beyond that something happens...it's a sort of spiritual experience...Your range of vision is very narrow, which is the same for most costumes. That adds to the sense of delirium.'

He also used photography to explore other aspects of his characters' personalities, often revealing a more private self through placing them in unexpected situations, such as the macho Tom in a face pack scrubbing the kitchen floor.

For Heath-Kerr, the impetus to make a costume began with a major event such as the Mardi Gras or an exhibition opening and the character revolved around the image he wished to project there. 'I've tried as much as possible to give them a longer lifespan than just one event. Of course, when I first started they were things I only wore for the party then trashed.'

Heath-Kerr believed his lack of formal art training enabled his particular form of art to develop because he did not have the restriction of thinking about what should or should not be done.

Brenton Heath-Kerr died of an AIDS-related illness in 1995. He was 33.

Glamour on a shoestring

by Judith O'Callaghan

'The early days of the workshop were somewhere between Santa's workshop, with tons of glitter and colour and sequins and beautiful objects, and a rat's nest'. Ron Smith[1]

From fairly tenuous beginnings in the early 1980s, it has been the Sydney Gay & Lesbian Mardi Gras Workshop—through its volunteers and paid employees—that has helped shape the look and feel of the parade and parties. In addition, it has given its services to other Mardi Gras events and supplied designs for commercial projects. The role of the workshop, however, is larger than the scope of its production. It was established with the idea of involving gay men and lesbians in a creative community-based activity that promoted the development and sharing of skills, as well as a sense of pride, achievement and identity. While the workshop's management and culture may have changed over the last 14 years, this principle has remained constant.

Photo: William Yang, 1987

When a giant puppet-like figure resembling Imelda Marcos appeared in the 1987 parade, tearfully chasing dozens of large shoes on poles, it was an instant hit with the crowd. No-one recognised her as a clever product of the workshop's recycling policy. 'Imelda' was, in fact, a re-worked 'Babs Divine', who had had a nasty experience in an earlier, wetter parade when she took on too much water through her sponge-rubber 'skin'.

Workshop artist Brett Grant hard at work over a tonne of tulle. A large part of the job for the team of casually-employed artists is to give shape to the ideas that parade participants bring to the workshop. As senior workshop artist Ian McMillan explains: 'They have to enhance their ideas rather than destroy them...allowing for diversity...and providing different levels of assistance'.

'It's a very social place where a lot of conflicts are resolved, where gay men and lesbians manage to get over their differences, where people find out about each other as well as getting a lot of skills.' Ian McMillan, Senior Workshop Artist[2]

Today the workshop attracts a broad spectrum of gay men and lesbians to its new facilities within the SGLMG offices in Sydney's inner west. In the ten-week season leading up to Mardi Gras 1996, over 100 volunteers and about 50 groups made use of its services. For some time now, the volunteers have included not only Sydneysiders, but also interstate and international visitors. As one English volunteer explains:

'We know that it's the biggest event that happens in the world...we know there is nothing to compare to this. It's difficult to get here just for Mardi Gras so there's a lot of excitement. I'm going to bore everyone silly on the day, going "I did that bit".'[3]

For the rest of the year, apart from the five-week Sleaze season (see Chapter 1) and the servicing of external commissions, the workshop is there for 'anyone to use it'—from a gay or lesbian artist needing a large space to work to a group that wants to borrow props for a special occasion.

In terms of the parade itself, the workshop's core responsibilities are to provide advice and assistance on entries, produce components such as floats and props, and provide some kind of order or shape to the event. Despite pressure at various times from within the organisation, any 'unifying' themes for Mardi Gras have been treated rather loosely, the priority being self-expression.

'We don't set a theme or dictate to anybody what they can do...you can wear thongs and stubbies in the parade if you want to.' Ian McMillan

Nevertheless, bringing it all together for the big night presents a very particular kind of challenge:

'From a design point of view the Sydney Gay & Lesbian Mardi Gras...[is] approached as a many-headed monster, a problem to be attacked on many fronts. As a piece of street theatre, it has to be both political and spectacular; as a medium of expression, it has to be aesthetic as well as intellectual, and on all levels completely free of censorship. It must be cost effective as well as extravagant. It must be contradictory and inclusive. It is both an overall problem—the considerations that apply to the whole parade, the route, the crowd, the big picture—and a collection of individual problems—the individual and group entries—which may have very little to do with each other thematically.' Ian McMillan

'The workshop was for getting people together.' Bill Whittaker

For the 1995 parade, a group of lesbians running their own businesses in Melbourne, transported the parts of their 'Lezbiz' float—a giant cash-register—to the workshop for assembly. Different groups have different needs and the same year the main Aboriginal entry, the 'Everybody's Business' float, was made off-site using workshop materials and equipment as required.

Sydney Asian Lesbians used the workshop to make their float in 1995 and went on to win best community entrant in that year's Sydney Gay & Lesbian Mardi Gras awards. The float represented the marriage ceremony of two women in the style of a traditional Chinese wedding within a temple setting. The Chinese character held here means 'double happiness' but has been cleverly adapted to include a lesbian symbol.

As a way of assisting these individual and group entries, the workshop has produced its own 'Guidelines for floatmakers'. These range over all categories including 'single entry', 'the small free-ranging walking group', 'larger walking groups' and 'marching groups', as well as floats and props. It begins with some basic design pointers:

> *'The theme is the first thing to be worked out: then comes the visualisation of this theme, the "look", a calculated way of maximising visual impact. Draw it and plan it. From there, it's on to the realisation: making it work. This is largely a matter of attention to detail, practicalities, teamwork, organisation, and a great deal of common sense.'*

The guidelines also cover the types of vehicles that can be used, from eight-tonne trucks down to 'small pushables':

> *'It's always nice to have something to lean on during those exhausting last few hundred metres. Or you can give new meaning to the concept of drag, by dragging some of your favourite memorabilia with you. And they're so practical: as your costume crumbles you can add its pieces to your pushable/draggable prop!'*

If required, the workshop can provide further advice but in terms of physical access to the facility, both groups and individuals are invited to apply for space when they fill in their parade entry forms. The pressure of demand can be fierce, particularly in the weeks leading up to the parade when, according to senior workshop artist Ian McMillan, 'people are fighting over a square centimetre of space'.

While the workshop's role as a servicing agent for the parade has remained consistent over the years, there have been fundamental changes to its operation. Furthermore, its profile within the organisation has substantially altered; from being the flagship of Mardi Gras it has become just one part of a much larger whole. But then, not only has the Mardi Gras organisation changed, notions of 'community' have also changed. Although the annual Mardi Gras parade and festival might provide a rallying point, no one talks seriously any more about a single gay and lesbian community, other than in a political context or as a general term of description. So where does that leave enterprises, such as the SGLMG workshop, that have been established around that concept? What was a community workshop and what is it now?

The history of the Mardi Gras workshop begins in 1982, four years after the first parade. With the formation of the Gay Mardi Gras Committee, a strategy for developing the look of the parade emerged, which included the institution of the Sleaze Ball as a fundraiser for the event. One of the prime movers was Peter Tully, a Sydney-based jeweller and costume designer.

It appears that it was largely through Tully that a submission was made to the Australia Council (the federal arts funding body) for financial assistance with 'the implementation of an arts program' in support of the 1983 Mardi Gras parade. The application was successful, and although only $6,000 was granted, it provided the critical impetus.

> *'The reality is that workshop would not have happened and maybe even the Mardi Gras as it now is would never have happened without that support for Peter to run the workshop.' Bill Whittaker*[4]

Peter Tully had participated in the first Mardi Gras and was one of the few to have 'dressed' for the occasion. During 1979-1980 he travelled to New York on another Australia Council grant and the experience—most particularly of the city's gay subculture—broadened his own practice as well as strengthening and consolidating his ideas about the expression of cultural identity through art.

> *'Because I had an interest in native American art and the various tribes of Indians—and the African things, and I had my New Guinea experiences, I was looking at urban groups, the punks, blacks, Puerto Ricans, WASPS, Gays, and they were all little components of New York society and I more or less saw them as little tribes. And so I started making things for my tribe and drawing on my interest in real tribes;...at that stage my tribe was New York Gay...and I guess my tribe is still the Gay community. The Gay tribe.'*[5]

Tully had also seen the famous Greenwich Village Halloween Parade originated by puppeteer and theatre director Ralph Lee in 1974. Strongly supported by the local gay community, the parade was then still based around the spectacular puppets produced in Lee's loft.[6] Tully was apparently inspired by the experience. After returning home, he became involved with a workshop associated with the Festival of Sydney, producing among other things a giant Edna Everage puppet for a parade. When asked how he became interested in Mardi Gras, Tully replied:

> *'Well, if you were in Sydney at that time you couldn't really avoid it. It made a wonderful forum for the creativity that was getting wasted here in Sydney. I was on the committee so we were able to get money from the Australia Council using my name, because I had already exhibited quite widely in Sydney. It just sort of snowballed from there.'*[7]

Every person, prop, costume and float competes for the attention of the crowd and cameras, and so materials are selected for maximum impact. Colour and brightness are obvious considerations, whether in fluorescent paints, sequins or holigraphic paper.

Faggots
Against
Runway
Three
SOLVER
Flat Acrylic
Scenic Paint
FLUORESCENT
GREEN
W.P. Crowhurst Pty. Ltd. 37 Belford Avenue, Devon Park, Sth. Aust.

The position of artistic director—filled initially by Tully—was clearly defined: to involve and instruct people in the design and fabrication of props, floats, decorations and costumes for the parade, and to generally organise the look of the event and develop and supervise its unifying themes.

Tully's role was pivotal. His particular creative vision complemented the ambitions of the workshop as a gay and lesbian community arts enterprise. He believed that 'art should be for everyone' which was reflected in the sorts of materials he chose to use in his own work, such as mass-produced components, plastics, toys and kitchenware. His ideas about the development of a cultural identity for gay men and lesbians were also not limited by traditional models, with his own costume and jewellery again reflecting a mix of influences, from tribal cultures to Australian popular imagery. Art was meant to be enjoyed and Tully fully understood the power of humour in the context of events such as Mardi Gras:

> *'Art is a great tool and humour is a great tool too, and those things have been combined with the politics. I think that's why we've got such an effective parade with the images and icons that are created by the artists from the community, and that comes out of a shared experience.'*
> *Peter Tully*[8]

To assist with setting up the workshop, Tully brought in two artists he had met through the Festival of Sydney, Michael Doherty and Suzanne Holman, who had broad experience of community arts-based projects. He also used his connections within the wider arts network to secure the workshop's first location.[9] For the 12-week period leading up to the 1983 Mardi Gras, the workshop used the area beneath the Sydney Dance Company's rehearsal space in a warehouse located in Griffiths Street, Woolloomooloo, one of Sydney's oldest and toughest inner-city suburbs. 'It was hideous...a "carpark" and Mardi Gras had a corner', recalls Bill Whittaker who joined the workshop as a volunteer in 1982. It had its problems, including poor security, and the overhead lighting had to be rigged up from extension leads.

However inhospitable the surrounds, for the first time there was a large centralised location for the preparation of parade entries within striking distance of Oxford Street and the parade route. Letters were sent out in November to all known gay groups in Sydney advising them of the workshop and its services, so by the time the workshop commenced operation in December, there were more than enough people wanting to use the facility or volunteering labour and skills.

As artistic director, Tully's time was largely taken up with organising, directing and assisting, more than producing his own

Photo: William Yang, 1983

'Yoda' and friends at the workshop's first location in Woolloomooloo. This was one of the large costume pieces produced by the workshop for the 1983 parade. It was modelled in papier-mâché by Ross Hill (far right). In front are (left to right) artist Michael Doherty, an unknown artist/volunteer, artist Suzanne Holman, artistic director Peter Tully and volunteer Bill Whittaker.

designs. Money as well as time was at a premium, with the whole budget (including Tully's and the artists' salaries) amounting to only $8,200.[10] There was no alternative but to be inventive. 'Glamour on a shoestring' became the workshop's motto.

'I think it was an advantage not to have money in the start because we started with a squat for a workshop. We had to go to Reverse Garbage and find stuff off the street to create magic. The passion and intensity of everyone involved meant it was from the heart; it was strong. Now we have a little more money, it helps enormously but we also come from the strength of knowing we can do it with nothing.' David McDiarmid[11]

Reverse Garbage was—and still is—a major source of materials for parade props, floats and costumes for the parade. A commercial warehouse, it is a wonderful repository of industrial off-cuts and leftovers which can be bought cheaply by weight. Of course, a lot of scrounging and recycling went on as well to supplement the purchased materials. During the early years, apparently, Christmas decorations that had previously been used by Grace Bros department store were reworked for use in a number of parades:

'One of the tortures inflicted on new volunteers was the untangling and testing of the Christmas lights.' Ron Smith

As tools and equipment were also in short supply, production techniques were fairly basic. Flags, signs, street decorations and banners were screenprinted or hand-painted. Mass-produced components from Reverse Garbage were wired, taped, screwed or glued together for costumes and floats. The hot glue gun later became the mainstay for most productions and burning your hand on one became a rite of passage for workshop initiates, as artist Ron Smith recalls: 'We could only afford the cheap ones where you pushed the glue in with your hand, so you just waited for the yell'.

Opposite, top: The 1983 Mardi Gras parade was the first to benefit from the workshop's assistance. 'Thousands responded to the call for creativity and got themselves up as bikies, Darth Vaders, cycle sluts, gladiators, red Indians, Supremes, Carmen Mirandas, wizards, fairies, ballroom dancers, nuns and altar boys, with varying degrees of success and impact on the viewers. Others simply wore sufficient to keep them out of the Darlinghurst slammer on indecent exposure.' Sydney Morning Herald, *26 February 1983.*

'In the end it's street theatre. You can broadcast a whole lot of different messages. Efficiency doesn't always mean a good parade.' Peter Tully

Right: Ron Smith joined the workshop at the end of 1983 and was its artistic director from 1986 to 1988. Even after officially leaving, the workshop still held a strong attraction for him: 'Apart from the people, it was basically because, like so many queens, I spent a lot of my life escaping through fantasy and dreaming about creating something spectacular and glamorous like a Busby Berkeley production. And to actually come into a thing where you're allowed to realise your dreams is fantastic'.

Photo: C.Moore Hardy, 1990

Photo: William Yang, 1985

David McDiarmid (left) and Peter Tully (right) stepped out with 'Zippy', a Ron Smith creation, in the 1988 parade. The pun is a popular device for Mardi Gras designs, and the 'camp pie' carriable is one of a series of props produced by the workshop that played on the names of well-known products.

Apart from the glue guns, papier-mâché was about the most complex technology employed and it was used very effectively in the production of large puppet figures and masks. Among the most memorable designs from the 1983 parade were two large puppet-like costumes modelled on 'ET' and 'Yoda', skilfully crafted by artist Ross Hill who, legend has it, went on to join Bill Henson and the Muppets.

'We had very small budgets in the beginning. It's due to the ability and creativeness of some artists that we got such wonderful pieces in the early days. Perhaps not having any money made people more creative than perhaps they would normally be.' Peter Tully[12]

The 1983 Mardi Gras—the first to benefit from the workshop's support—was considered a great success. One of Sydney's main newspapers observed that the parade was 'awfully well organised' and 'thousands [had] responded to the call for creativity'.[13] Spurred on by the achievement, another grant submission was made to the Australia Council, but without success.[14] Nevertheless, there was enough commitment from the Gay Mardi Gras Committee for the workshop to be re-established for the 1984 season.

Ron Smith was among the volunteers who were attracted to Griffiths Street at the end of 1983. Originally trained as a painter at Sydney's National Art School, Smith had been involved in a number of co-operative artists' projects, including the infamous Roxy in Taylor Square—an anarchic artists' commune-come-studio-come-'playground' — in the early 1970s. For Smith, the workshop was an exciting place to be:

'I loved working with other people who were as driven to make mad items that were publicly seen. And the process of making the things, the actual workshopping of those things was so fabulous.'

But this was only the workshop's second season and for Smith a few things still needed to be resolved. A number of the paid artists were hired on a casual basis to work on specific projects, and in some cases their role as team leaders was not effectively performed. The fact that these artists were not necessarily gay, but employed for their skills and experience, was also an issue: 'Politically they didn't have anything to say'.

By the following season, it had all come together:

'1985 was a good year for people, both staff and volunteers...something jelled...It wasn't just that the people had skills, but that they had actually learnt to work together...I think that was probably the most important thing to happen and it showed that year and for many years after that.'

There had also been a change in venue. The workshop had moved to a two-storey 'derelict' warehouse at 49 Forbes Street, Woolloomooloo, literally around the corner. Parade props as well as boxes of materials had begun to accumulate and needed to be stored and secured.

'Over there is a giant pineapple and there's a slice of watermelon so large that if it were real the pips could be used for doorstops. Here is a construction that resembles in its unfinished stages the skeleton of an outsized fish and there an armless blue torso with a red peaked hat. Now, imagine a monstrous banana and you would be that much closer to the sights of the Mardi Gras Workshop...Upstairs a small band of volunteer workers hum and buzz. The old warehouse is alive with birds—parrots, to be more precise, their carmine red heads being stuck together with glue and paper over timber frames and chicken wire...In a large corner room...an industrial sewing machine is being operated busily by a brightly smiling enthusiast. Another, larger room has nothing much in it except for a big table covered in white paper with some of those well known pink triangle flags resting on it...Crouched on the floor a young man in dark glasses strains over what appears to be a graphic in indeterminate intention while in an adjacent almost hidden room lurks a large lump of polyurethane foam frescoed with little plastic growths.' Oxford Lifestyle Magazine, *February 1985*

A lot of energy that year was devoted to producing group displays such as the 'parrot' costumes, which reflected Tully's emphasis on creating massed effect at street level:

'Group displays are more effective and we are encouraging community groups to participate in this way as well as entering floats. I think this year the larger number of groups on foot will add to the colour of the parade. There will also be more music and percussion...and some surprises.'[15]

One of the brightly coloured 'parrot' costumes produced by the workshop for a group display in the 1985 Mardi Gras. An emphasis on imaginative 'walking' entries was part of an overall strategy to make the parade more engaging for spectators. 'In the last few years we've had some wonderful floats, but people became more passive and just stand there and watch the parade. That's not the idea. Mardi Gras is about participation'. Peter Tully, Star, *21 February 1985*

Photo: William Yang

Photo: Ron Smith, 1987

For Tully, dramatic effect was all important: 'We have the advantage of it being an evening parade and so it can be spectacular'.[16] Accordingly, he insisted on follow-spots along the parade route to reinforce that sense of theatre. But of course, there were never enough.

Tully's theatrical flair was given full rein when it was decided to develop a concept party for Sleaze 1985. This involved designing decor and sets for the large Hordern Pavilion venue in the Sydney Showgrounds.

> *'It was as if ancient Rome had collided with a Mayan city with Boy George as Shivah guarding the temple gates. Cecil B de Mille would have wept as the operatic-scale pageant swept through thousands of enthralled revellers.'* Star Observer, *18 October 1985*

Again all this had to be achieved on fairly meagre resources. Tools usually belonged to the people who used them or were hired on a needs basis. Tully supplied his own little tool kit, which according to Smith, was 'very tragic...a tack hammer, screwdriver, no power tools'. Apart from what was made in the workshop, columns were scrounged from the Australian Broadcasting Commission's prop department, while the giant skull that was used at the party entrance was winkled out of a prop-hire business at a bargain rate because the workshop was prepared to renovate it.

> *'We had to convert these huge bomb shelters into something really atmospheric or glamorous, or whatever the theme was...we always had a fairly tight budget so...things had to be thought out and lit properly and accentuated.' Peter Tully*[17]

The 1985 Sleaze set a benchmark, not just for future Sleaze balls, but for dance parties around Sydney. The Mardi Gras party, however, fell into a different category. While the workshop did eventually provide decor and sets for the party's various shows and venues at the Showgrounds, a 'concept' seemed rather superfluous given that the party was meant as an extension of the parade. In any case, originating and realising a concept for Sleaze on an annual basis placed an extra demand on the workshop and so its period of operation was extended from three to six months, with the season beginning in September and running straight through until the end of February.

Famous drag artist Doris Fish, on stilts in the Forbes Street workshop, trying on an oversized costume for the 1987 parade. Adjusting her trim is John McDowell, who worked in the wardrobe departments of the National Institute of Dramatic Art (NIDA) and the Australian Opera as well as running his own costume design studio.

The 1986 parade was again 'bigger than ever' and according to the report submitted to the Australia Council, more emphasis had been placed on the parade route. In addition to the street decorations and lighting, the workshop had also provided advice on pyrotechnics and arranged a laser display in Oxford and Flinders Streets. But the phenomenal growth of the parade had its associated costs:

'It is only through the artists' energy and personal commitment to Mardi Gras, and the working of exceptionally long hours (often to the workers' social detriment) that the projects were completed. It is nearly impossible to complete such an ambitious project in such a limited time and retain a high standard...We are almost victims of our own success.' Australia Council Artistic Report, *1986*

In recognition of this increasing workload, the committee of what was now the Sydney Gay Mardi Gras Association Inc agreed to make the artistic director's position a 12-month full-time job in 1987. Ron Smith, who had taken over from Tully in directing the 1986 Sleaze, assumed the mantle: 'I became artistic director partly because Peter liked what I was doing and he was overwhelmed with other work. He was doing major exhibits and travelling overseas and wanted to hand the baton on to someone he trusted'. Tully nevertheless remained a strong and visible presence within the workshop for some time to come. In fact, it became common for artists to retain a close association with the workshop, even after quite traumatic estrangements.

Smith was not only visually creative, but also highly skilled in a range of processes such as vacuum-forming and various other plastics technologies. He introduced these 'butchy things' into the workshop's repertoire making it possible to construct some of the more physically ambitious designs. One of these was the 5.5 metre 'Tom of Finland' that featured in the 1988 parade. Made in fibreglass over a framework of electrical conduit, chicken-wire and foam, this gigantic figure went well above the height restrictions on parade entries: 'We had to have people running alongside him with poles to hold up the overhead power cables'.

Apart from the occasional indulgence, Smith had a very down-to-earth approach to the production of parade designs, particularly in terms of the kinds of conditions that they could face during the course of the event. In the '1987 Mardi Gras guide', he provided some practical advice to participants:

'The Parade route follows the windy rise between the harbour and Botany Bay so anchor those wigs well, and perforate banners so they won't break or blow away. Don't risk becoming a walking wettex—waterproof your costume. Use synthetic fabrics—they don't hold water. Cover cardboard with clear Contact paper. Use waterproof glues

Photo: William Yang, 1988

The paintings of Picasso provided one of the most impressive visual themes of the 1988 parade. Some of the artist's most famous works, such as 'Weeping woman' and 'Portrait of Gertrude Stein' were brought to life in a series of costumes, made from foamcore and polystyrene and painted by Tony Priddle. Here a headpiece from one of the costumes rests on the floor of the workshop, while a 'skirt' is adjusted on its wearer.

Photo: C.Moore Hardy, 1990

Ian Oliver, Mandy Smith and Githa Pilbrow with the set of fancy cowboy boot carriables they produced for a lesbian group entry in the 1990 parade. Smith was the first lesbian artist employed by the workshop and when she was approached about developing a theme for the group, she chose country and western: 'Dykes have always been into C & W so I thought we might as well make a public demonstration of it'.

and paints. Protect generators and wiring from water to avoid short circuits and electrocution. And don't put anything flammable—especially the spare petrol—on or near the generator or lights.'

The other full-time position created during this period was that of executive director, which was meant, in part, to take the administrative load off the workshop. From the beginning there was tension between the position and the artists. Until now, the workshop had been largely left to itself.

'It operated in a fairly anarchic manner—members of the committee rarely visited the workshop. We were simply allocated money—a very, very small amount of money—and the cash was kept in a honey jar on the desk, and anybody who needed money for materials took money from the jar and went and bought the materials and replaced the money with a receipt, hopefully.' Ron Smith

This began to change, and what was described by the committee as responsible management was perceived by the artists as unnecessary and uninformed interference in their area of expertise. As the administrative side of the organisation increased over subsequent years, the relationship between the committee and the workshop progressively deteriorated. One of the first public expressions of this growing dissension was Tully's resignation from the committee in January 1988.

To offset the cost of the two full-time salaries, 'limited commercial use' of the workshop was established. One of its first contracts was to hire out some its existing props to World Expo 88 in Brisbane while another involved the production of toy grenadier guard costumes in hard plastic for the Military Tattoo. Over the next few years, an increasing emphasis was placed on developing the commercial side of the workshop as a means of justifying its operation on a year-round basis. Before long, it was expected to pay at least part of its own way, by earning a specified income.

By the 1988 Mardi Gras, the workshop had moved into larger premises in 187 Boundary Street, Rushcutters Bay, including offices that were gradually filled by more administrative staff. The parade itself was seen to represent a broader diversity of gay men and lesbians. It was the first year that an Aboriginal float had been entered, for example, and it was also the first appearance of Dykes on Bikes, heralding a greater level of participation by lesbians in Mardi Gras overall.

For most of the workshop's early history, there appears to have been no lesbian involvement in terms of either paid or volunteer staff. Most lesbians had left the organisation by the time the workshop was established, although some still participated in the parade and used the facilities to make and construct their entries. Efforts were apparently made to encourage lesbians to be more involved, but even Ron Smith admits that there was 'bugger-all camaraderie' on the floor and some women were left with the impression that they were not particularly welcome. Gradually, however, the dynamic changed as lesbians began to join the workshop as volunteers and in November 1988, Mandy Smith became the first to be employed as an artist.

Smith had met Peter Tully while working on Expo 88 and it was he who persuaded her to join the workshop: 'You were hand-picked as part of the family'.[18] She remembers the 1989 Mardi Gras season as being 'fantastic but traumatic'. On one hand, relations with the committee were becoming increasingly strained, on the one other, the creative energy of the workshop was at a peak. Artist and designer David McDiarmid, who was just back after years of working in the USA, had taken over from Ron Smith as artistic director and Canadian Jeffrey Douglas was the other paid artist.

Apart from sharing a similarly 'bent' sense of humour, McDiarmid, Douglas and Mandy Smith complemented each other in terms of their individual strengths. McDiarmid was conceptually daring and inventive and was the first to bring a computer into the workshop. Predominantly used for generating graphics, the initiative tied in well with Mardi Gras' push to develop its corporate identity and promotional activities. Jeffrey Douglas had come to the workshop as a volunteer with no arts background or experience but under Ron Smith's guidance had developed great skill in working with plastics such as fibreglass and polystyrene.

The loss of Ron Smith, however, had left a large gap in the area of practical construction skills and problem solving, which Mandy Smith with her background in scenic design ably filled: 'The men couldn't build anything!'. Such a division of roles was not uncommon in the workshop. As Ron Smith observed:

> *'Dykes always bought their own tools—the heavy-duty stuff like circular saws that no queen ever had or knew what to do with.'*

As for the rest of the workshop, many of the old guard such as Peter Tully and Doris Fish were still around, but there was also new blood and a new dynamic: 'all the tribal groupings were there working together'. Among the recent inductees were Brian Ross (an architectural model-maker) and Philippa Playford (still a student at Sydney College of the Arts). This creative team of artists and volunteers produced some remarkable designs for the 1989 parade, from Fred Nile's 'head' to the float, costumes, carriables and 'robot' developed for the Tin Toy-Space theme. For artists like Playford, the experience fed and enriched their own work:

Photo: William Yang, 1989

One of the most memorable carriables in the history of the parade was an effigy of the head of the Reverend Fred Nile—a fierce opponent of Mardi Gras—surrounded by the Sisters of Perpetual Indulgence. Richly detailed, it was modelled in papier-mâché by workshop artist Jeffrey Douglas, with make-up by Doris Fish. 'Fred Nile has earned a place because he has done so much to support and publicise the Mardi Gras,' Sister Turnover said. 'We thought we should give him this token of our thanks.' Sydney Morning Herald, *20 February 1989.*

'My training has been art school training, a Bachelor of Visual Arts mostly in glass...The Mardi Gras workshop and the artists...opened my mind to other materials...sort of freed up the camper side of my work...Just the fact that I was around so many incredible artists that were so strong and brave in their artwork and had a real boldness to their whole persona...really influenced me and supported me developing as an artist.'[19]

While strong relationships frequently developed among the artists, the rift between them and the organising committee was growing. Factionalism has always dogged or propelled Mardi Gras, depending on your point of view, and by this stage the workshop had evolved into a faction within the organisation. A 'reform ticket', largely generated by the artists and Peter Tully, was submitted for the election of the 1989-1990 committee. It gained nine of the 14 positions, which included Cath Phillips as President. However, the new broom was not quite what the workshop expected.

'Everyone got caught up with ideas of excellence. Old leftie-style organisations were no longer considered viable.' Mandy Smith

Sydney Gay & Lesbian Mardi Gras Inc was no longer the tiny organisation that it had been back in the early 1980s. It now had a turnover of almost $1,000,000 so tighter management and financial control was a necessity. At the same time, more emphasis was placed on the workshop drawing in outside contracts to pay its way. By the middle of 1989, the artists were already very busy, completing work on major parties (Pride and Birthday 1 & 2) as well as providing production assistance on four others.

'Our prop-hire division has rented props to various advertising agencies, film productions and Macquarie University. The art department has been contracted to design an exhibition poster, a bookjacket for Black Wattle Press and a mural for the Preterm Foundation.' Newsletter No 5, *July 1989*

The strategy to accelerate this side of the operation included the appointment of Di Henry, who was given overall responsibility for the workshop after David McDiarmid's contract was not renewed. Di Henry was neither an artist nor a lesbian, but was chosen on the basis of her management skills. As Cath Phillips recalled: 'We didn't want a great artist, we wanted a great manager'.[20] By October 1990, the workshop had produced props and sets for a number of nightclubs, sculptures and posters for the Travel Industry Awards, oversized bouquet awards for the International Year of Literacy and a number of items for the Grace Bros parade. While all this provided employment to artists associated with

The HIV Support Group's 199 parade entry was designed b David McDiarmid in the 'styl of a Mexican skeleton, simila to the Day of the Dead feast According to McDiarmid, som people were negative abou using an image of death for group that is about life. 'But th other half of the group felt tha to own an image was to den the power of a negative image.

Photo: C. Moore Hardy, 1992

Workshop artist Lea Adams painting the legend 'Remember Our Friends' for the 1995 Remembrance Event float

the workshop, it also brought in outside specialists who were not necessarily in accord with the ethos of the place.

The overall shift in direction for the workshop undoubtedly caused some difficulties for the artists. More changes occurred within the staff. Jeffrey Douglas had gone back to Canada in 1989; David McDiarmid, who had returned as 'parade designer' at the end of 1989, left during the following year; while Mandy Smith had decided her 'use-by date had passed' after Mardi Gras 1990. Morale was also directly affected by the impact of the HIV/AIDS epidemic. By the early 1990s, many of those closely associated with the workshop had been diagnosed as HIV positive, including Peter Tully, David McDiarmid, Doris Fish and Brian Ross.

Then at the end of 1991, there was a crisis in management. Just as preparations for the 1992 Mardi Gras were stepping up, the general manager and then the workshop manager resigned, placing enormous pressure on everyone involved with the event. Subsequently the future of the workshop came under review and although Tully, McDiarmid and senior artist Githa Pilbrow tried to have the position of artistic director re-established, a completely new structure was decided upon.

The job of instituting the new regime was given to Katrina Marton, who had joined the organisation as events manager in 1991. Marton was made production manager in July 1992 and given overall responsibility for the workshop facilities and staff as well as the production of the parade, party and all major Mardi Gras events.[21] Artists were only to be employed on a casual basis on specific projects. The exception was the full-time position of senior workshop artist who was to facilitate the workshop's operation rather than originate and choose its artistic production. These creative responsibilities were taken over by the committees directly concerned with organising the major events, notably the parade and parties. Essentially the workshop was now defined as a service: to follow the artistic direction set by the committees and meet the needs of those gay men and lesbians who sought assistance from the facility.

These measures effectively established a new culture within the workshop. When the artists were informed of the changes, they completed work on Sleaze 1992 then left. Earlier in August, news had hit that Peter Tully had died in Paris from an AIDS-related illness. The Tully era had come to an end.

In December 1992, Ian McMillan—who had never met Peter Tully—was asked to take on the role of senior workshop artist, a position he still retains. McMillan's background is in visual and scenic art and the practical model he has adopted for the workshop is the one he knew in the theatre. Instead of a play's director, there is the committee with whom McMillan works to develop a design brief. From this, he produces a 'visualisation' within the limits of the workshop's capabilities, which may involve brainstorming sessions with people on the relevant subcommittees. The chosen designs are then executed by gay and lesbian artists from a loyal team that McMillan has assembled over the years. The other role of these artists is to provide assistance and advice to those individuals and groups who use the workshop.

Although McMillan is directly involved in establishing the order of the parade, these days the workshop's overall contribution is limited to producing the lead entry, the Remembrance Event and the costume and props for three marching groups. Like the Mardi Gras poster, the design of the lead entry is opened to outside artists, who are asked to submit designs for consideration by a committee. Depending on the particular skills of the chosen designer, he or she is encouraged to become directly involved in the production of the entry at the workshop. Em Owen, for example, was there to oversee the construction of her float but also to lend a hand with the 100 costumes that were required for her scheme 'Love and Chaos' in the 1996 parade.

For some people, this new arrangement means that the community, as represented through Sydney Gay & Lesbian Mardi Gras and its committees, remains in control of the workshop, not a minority of artists.

> *'We have changed the emphasis from a sort of tempestuous, indulgent, romantic, artistic vision to a more professional, reliable get-the-job-done approach. No private agendas.' Ian McMillan*

And, there are those who are critical of the 'new order', who believe the creative diversity of the workshop artists, their originality, their personal style provided the edge to Mardi Gras.

> *'What a lot of people forget about Mardi Gras is that it's the marriage of art and politics. The artist's role is crucial to Mardi Gras to present a sense of who we are—and that in itself is a political stand if you are a gay artist, whether it's a man or a woman.' David McDiarmid*

In anyone's terms, however, the Sydney Gay & Lesbian Mardi Gras workshop is an extraordinary enterprise that has no real parallel anywhere else in the world. Its significance stems not only from the art and design that it produces, but also its larger potential:

> *'In terms of developing a consciousness of what the gay and lesbian community is about, a consciousness of political issues, a consciousness of what we might need to fight for, of what we might need to do, it is a very important place for the fermentation of those ideas and for the education of a lot of people who come into it... The workshop was for getting people together from the very fragile community it was in those early years...and it can still play that part.' Bill Whittaker*

Photo: C. Moore Hardy, 1996

The 1996 lead entry 'Love and Chaos' was designed by Sydney artist Em Owen. It involved around 100 participants of varying ages, ethnic backgrounds and body types, in a processional dance around a luminous angel that 'represented the triumphant spirit, love and solidarity, rising above adversity'. The glow emanating from the towering winged figure was created by lights set within its steel framework and diffused by its Lycra skin.

Chapter 1

1. Ken Davis, speaking on an ABC Radio National documentary, 'I'll never hide again', 21 and 23 February 1993.
2. Craig Johnston. Interview with J O'Callaghan, 1995. All subsequent quotes are from this interview.
3. Craig Johnston, ibid.
4. David McDiarmid in *Feed them to the cannibals!*, video, Dangerous to Know, 1993.
5. Peter Tully in *Feed them to the cannibals!*, op cit.
6. Raymond, Leigh, 'Without you, I'm nothing—some reflections on the meaning of Stonewall', catalogue essay from the exhibition, Out with Pride: celebrating Stonewall 25, bare gAllery, Newtown, NSW, 23 June-3 July 1994.
7. Although Mardi Gras has had themes for the parade and festival, they do not generally impact visually on the parade. Any visual links usually happen as oblique references to the poster of that year. The themes are generally used as a means of galvanising the community and to hang a media message.
8. Peter Tully in *Feed them to the cannibals!*, op cit.
9. The worst example of sensational and false media reporting was perhaps that of *The Sydney Morning Herald* in its article 'AIDS victims watch as the parade goes by' on 25 February. It contained several untrue statements that led to a full retraction, apology and dismissal of the journalist responsible.
10. 'Gays risk AIDS at Mardi Gras', *Daily Sun*, Brisbane, 1 February 1985.
11. '1985 Mardi Gras parade', *The Star*, Vol 6, No 13, 20 December 1984, p 2.
12. Philippa Playford. Interview with J O'Callaghan, 18 July 1995.

Chapter 2

1. Philippa Playford. Interview with J O'Callaghan, 18 July 1995. All subsequent quotations from Playford are from this source.
2. Ron Muncaster. Interview with G Jones, 26 June, 1995. All subsequent quotations from Muncaster are from this source.
3. Brenton Heath-Kerr. Interview with J O'Callaghan, 12 May 1994. All subsequent quotations from Heath-Kerr are from this source.
4. Peter Tully and David McDiarmid in *Feed them to the cannibals!*, video, Dangerous to Know, 1993. All subsequent quotations from McDiarmid are from this source.
5. Kimberly O'Sullivan. Interview with J O'Callaghan and G Jones, 3 May 1995.
6. Vicki Jones. Interview with J O'Callaghan, 11 January 1996.
7. Happy Ho. Telephone conversation with J O'Callaghan, 28 July 1996.

Chapter 3

1. Ron Smith. Interview with J O'Callaghan, 11 January 1995, 21 June 1996 and telephone conversations in July-August 1996. All subsequent quotations from Smith are from these sources.
2. Ian McMillan. Interview with J O'Callaghan, 4 July 1996 and correspondence 13 August 1996. All subsequent quotations from McMillan are from these sources.
3. Workshop volunteer. Interview with R Swieca, 2 March 1994.
4. Bill Whittaker (Chairman/President, Sydney Gay Mardi Gras Association 1985-1986). Interview with G Jones, J O'Callaghan and R Swieca, 30 August 1995. All subsequent quotations from Whittaker are from this source.
5. Peter Tully quoted in John McPhee and Susan McCormack, *Peter Tully: Urban Tribalwear and Beyond*, exhibition catalogue, Australian National Gallery, Canberra, 1991.
6. By the late 1980s, Ralph Lee had disassociated himself from the parade because he believed it had become too big and had lost a sense of its origins, particularly its connection to the Greenwich Village community.
7. 'Peter Tully: Interview by Chris Dobney', *Outrage*, May 1987.
8. Peter Tully in *Feed them to the cannibals!*, video, Dangerous to Know, 1993.
9. During 1982, Tully had designed costumes and sets for Hate, a Sydney Dance Company ballet.
10. Australia Council grant plus $2200 from the Gay Mardi Gras Committee.
11. David McDiarmid in *Feed them to the cannibals!* All subsequent quotations from McDiarmid are from this source.
12. Peter Tully in *Feed them to the cannibals!*
13. Leo Schofield, 'Gay Mardi Gras outstrips Moomba', *Sydney Morning Herald*, 26 February 1983.
14. In total, the Community Arts Board of the Australia Council awarded five grants: 1982/83, 1984/85, 1985/86, 1986/87, 1987/88.
15. Peter Tully quoted in Denis Gallagher and Ian Barbour, 'Peter Tully at the Workshop', *Oxford Lifestyle Magazine*, 14 February 1985.
16. Peter Tully quoted in 'Workshop Gears up for Spectacular Mardi Gras', *Star*, 21 February 1985.
17. McPhee & McCormack, op cit.
18. Mandy Smith. Telephone conversation with J O'Callaghan, 16 July 1996. All subsequent quotations from Smith are from this source.
19. Philippa Playford. Interview with J O'Callaghan, 18 July 1995.
20. Cath Phillips. Interview with by G Jones, J O'Callaghan and R Swieca, 8 May 1995.
21. Katrina Marton. Interview with J O'Callaghan, 17 July 1996.

Other quotes

All quotes in this book that have not been footnoted are taken from the following sources:

Brenton Heath-Kerr. Interview with J O'Callaghan, 12 May 1994.
Craig Johnston. Interview with J O'Callaghan, 1995.
David McDiarmid. From *Feed them to the cannibals!*, video, Dangerous to Know, 1993.
Ian McMillan. Interview with J O'Callaghan, 4 July 1996 and correspondence 13 August 1996.
Ron Muncaster. Interview with G Jones, 26 June, 1995.
Philippa Playford. Interview with J O'Callaghan, 18 July 1995.
Ron Smith. Interview with J O'Callaghan, 11 January 1995, 21 June 1996 and telephone conversations in July-August 1996.
Peter Tully. From *Feed them to the cannibals!*, video, Dangerous to Know, 1993.
Bill Whittaker. Interview with G Jones, J O'Callaghan and R Swieca, 30 August 1995.